In memory of a YOUNG OCEAN EXPLORER...
BOBBY STAFFORD-BUSH
If you want to know more about Bobby's life check out:
www.bobbystaffordbush.co.nz

ISBN 978-0-473-30922-0

LOVE OUR OCEAN

YOUNG OCEAN EXPLORERS

93

LOVE OUR OCEAN

YOUNG OCEAN EXPLORERS

FOREWORD

"I was five years old when I first watched The Little Mermaid and decided my life's goal was to make friends with a talking fish and a well-spoken crab. I'd grown up near, on, and around the ocean, and came to understand it would be the only place I really felt at home. At seven years old, I was lucky to live on board a yacht and eventually learn to SCUBA dive. I came as close as I could to being a mermaid.

My favourite things to do as a child revolved around music and the ocean. In music, I drew inspiration from my experiences living on the sea and my understanding of what it meant to be a sailor. In my teen years I experienced my first real ocean crossing. Knowing what it feels like to completely leave the land and put your faith in the ocean is why I grew to develop a passion for keeping it safe.

I was lucky to get the opportunity in 2014 to work alongside Celine Cousteau, helping with turtle conservation in Costa Rica. We talked about conservation, science, environmental issues, but the most valuable message I took away from her was, 'instead of focusing constantly on what is wrong with the world, it's more helpful to shine a light on those who are doing something to help'. That's the light I want to shine on Riley and Steve.

As a young child, I had my father to show me the ropes when it came to the ocean and I appreciate that few children grow up the way I did. That's why I'm so excited about this project. Riley is here to show young people what the ocean is all about and, most importantly, teach them to love it too. Caring for the future of the ocean all starts with a spark of interest in the joy that it can bring a person.

Steve and Riley, and the entire Hathaway family are inspirations to me. I see Young Ocean Explorers as the beginning of the generation that saves the ocean"

JAMIE McDELL

check out all the cool illustrations Jamie's drawn throughout the book... she's also an award winning singer/songwriter

CONTENTS

WELCOME TO RILEY'S ADVENTURES	06	TURTLES	82
STINGRAYS / EAGLERAYS	08	TURTLE RESCUE	90
HARBOURS	16	MAKE A DIFFERENCE	91
CRAYFISH	26	SHARKS	92
ORCA	34	MARINE RESERVES	100
TRIPLEFINS	42	PHOTOGRAPHY GURU	102
BEHIND THE SCENES OF YOUNG OCEAN EXPLORERS	50	SNORKELLING'S FUN!	103
SANDAGERS WRASSE	52	GLOSSARY	104
ABOUT MY DAD	60	KICKSTARTER	106
COMMON DOLPHINS	62		
KELP	72		
93PERCENT	80		

LOVE OUR OCEAN

LOVE OUR OCEAN 06 YOUNG OCEAN EXPLORERS

HI! I'M RILEY HATHAWAY... YOUNG OCEAN EXPLORER and welcome to my adventures!

I can't imagine a life that didn't involve the ocean! With a dad that absolutely loves the water, we've been really lucky. We've grown up thinking that it's normal to have crayfish and fish for dinner – and we've seen some really amazing things, like pods of orca and dolphins in the bay just in front of our house!

Joining Dad on these Young Ocean Explorers adventures has made the last year the most amazing of my life. It's always been exciting hearing about what Dad got up to underwater, but to suddenly be there beside him doing it together...

IT'S BEEN AWESOME!

The idea for Young Ocean Explorers started when I chose a project at school about looking after the ocean. Sea turtles are one of my favourite animals and I'd heard they accidentally eat plastic that is floating in the ocean... so it was an easy choice really! I interviewed Dad's friend who's an expert on turtles and we added in some of Dad's video footage. I got an excellence grade for my project – YESSSSS!!! (Dad actually thinks he deserved it coz he helped with the project.) But way more exciting was the response we got when my project was played to my brother Dylan's year 6 class. His whole class loved the video and afterwards they couldn't stop talking about it! A couple of weeks later Dad asked me if I'd like to make more videos about marine animals... and... of course I said YES!!!

Straightaway, my mind was racing with all the other animals I'd love to find out more about – like dolphins, orca and stingrays. This was the start of Young Ocean Explorers!

I'd never have guessed how amazing this whole adventure would turn out to be. We've seen some of the ocean's biggest, scariest and most amazing creatures in real life! The underwater world is so magical – I hope that after reading this book, you'll want to put on a mask and snorkel and become a...

YOUNG OCEAN EXPLORER.

AOTEAROA – NEW ZEALAND
HAURAKI GULF
LITTLE BARRIER
AUCKLAND

LOVE OUR OCEAN

YOUNG OCEAN EXPLORERS

WHAI / WHAI KEO

STINGRAYS / EAGLE RAYS

DASYATIS THETIDIS
MYLIOBATIS TENUICAUDATUS

LOVE OUR OCEAN / YOUNG OCEAN EXPLORERS 09

WHAI / WHAI KEO
STINGRAYS / EAGLE RAYS
DASYATIS THETIDIS
MYLIOBATIS TENUICAUDATUS

"I'd always wanted to go to Little Barrier Island, coz Dad told me that it looks like the island out of the movie Jurassic Park!"

I wasn't expecting to see any dinosaurs on this trip, although we were heading out to look for a creature that has been around for a very long time – the stingray!

We had Dr Agnes Le Port on the boat with us; she's an expert on stingrays and eagle rays. As we headed out to Little Barrier, little did we know that we were in for a MASSIVE surprise! About halfway out, there was a sudden splash right beside the boat. Looking pretty excited, Dad spun the boat around, looking for the animal we had startled. Just then a huge shape, about the size of a large trampoline swam past the boat, it was a MANTA RAY, a creature that's hardly ever seen in New Zealand! Even Dr Le Port had never seen one in New Zealand before, and she has been working with rays here for over seven years!

Eagle ray

Long-tailed stingray

DID YOU KNOW?... In breeding season the teeth of male rays and skates become sharp, which allows them to grip the female during mating. After breeding season the male's teeth go back to being a flat shape.

It glided past us with the tips of its huge wings rising, breaking the glassy water. Dad quickly grabbed his camera and jumped in, swimming after it. I couldn't believe what I was seeing...

WOW!

...here we were coming out here to look for stingrays and eagle rays and instead, we had seen the biggest ray of them all! Dad was so excited when he got out of the water – the manta swam right up to him! He reckons the ocean is really cool like that – there's always the possibility of something unreal happening!

DID YOU KNOW?... Both eagle rays and stingrays are viviparous, which means they give birth to a small number of fully formed young after 4-9 months gestation (just like us).

When we got to Little Barrier it was really beautiful just like Dad had said: it's New Zealand's oldest nature reserve, and predator-free. There are so many birds there that you can hear them singing across the ocean. Entering the water, it was even more incredible; the water was clear and there were lots of eagle rays and long-tail stingrays lazing around in the shallows. Maybe they were relaxing before dinnertime!?

I LIKE MY SPACE NR.

DID YOU KNOW?... Eagle rays have even been known to leap out of the water when being chased by predators like orca.

I was worried about their barbed tails, but Dr Le Port said rays only use their tails when they're frightened or in defense from a predator. They normally only sting people if they get stood on; then they sometimes flick their tail up in defense, which can cause a painful injury.

Dr Le Port says eagle rays and stingrays are related to each other but look quite different. Eagle rays are diamond-shaped, with pointy wings, and stingrays look more like a kite with rounded wings. They swim quite differently too! Eagle rays fly like birds through the water, flapping their wings and can shoot like lightning through the shallows if scared or being chased. Stingrays look more like a rippling magic carpet. They are super-graceful.

DID YOU KNOW?... Eagle rays flush prey out of the sand by drawing in water through the small openings behind their eyes and blasting it through their gills.

WHAI / WHAI KEO

STINGRAYS / EAGLE RAYS

DASYATIS THETIDIS
MYLIOBATIS TENUICAUDATUS

LOVE OUR OCEAN   YOUNG OCEAN EXPLORERS

12

Short-tailed stingray

Something crazy about stingrays and eagle rays is that their eyes are on the top side of their heads and their mouths are on the underneath side. This seems so weird but it lets them watch for predators while they eat. Rays move around on the sea floor to search for food but instead of using sight, they use a sixth sense: they can detect the weak electrical fields that are given off by other animals.

Rays really do need eyes in the back of their head because they are food for orca AND sharks! In particular, orca have got ray-hunting sussed. They know to pick a ray up by the wing or the tip of the tail, avoiding those barbs. They've also figured out that when rays get turned upside down they fall into a trance-like state. Dad says this is called 'tonic immobility'. He's filmed orca heaps of times as they turn upside down while approaching the target; grabbing the ray in their mouths and flipping it back around to put it into a trance. It makes it much easier for the orca to eat the ray - there's no wriggling - it's a zombie! I reckon it's sooooo clever of orca to figure this out!

I FEEL SO SLEEPY

During the last snorkel of the day, Dr Le Port suddenly yelled...

SHARK!!!!

What?? Freaking out, I jumped straight onto dad's back. I didn't know how big the shark was or why it was coming around us! Then out of the corner of my eye I saw it: it was a bit bigger than me and looked amazing – I quickly got off dad's back and swam after it to have a closer look. It really didn't seem interested in us and soon swam out of sight.

MAN THAT WAS COOL!

This was my most amazing day ever in the ocean – seeing a manta, swimming with long-tail rays and eagle rays - and then to have a shark swim past. Wow, I'm still buzzing out! I had no idea this much amazing life lived so close to the mainland.

THIS IS ONE DAY I WILL NEVER FORGET!

Meet the Gurus

STINGRAY GURU
AGNÈS LE PORT

Nationality? French & New Zealand.

Do you have any hobbies? Scuba diving, hiking, stand-up paddle boarding, gardening, sewing and cooking.

Why did you decide to be a scientist? Children look at the world in wonder and want explanations about why and how things work the way they do. I never grew out of asking 'why' and I knew by the time I was 14 that I wanted to be a marine biologist.

How long have you been working in science? About 15 years.

Did you enjoy school and did you find learning easy? I loved school. I am a very competitive person and wanting to be the best pushed me to study hard. But like most students, there were some subjects I was good at (biology) and some that I struggled with (maths).

Where do you work? I have just left the University of Auckland where I had studied and worked since 2001 and have moved to sunny North Queensland to work at James Cook University in Townsville, near the Great Barrier Reef.

What do you do? I am very lucky to have a very varied work life. One aspect is showcasing the amazing research which is being done by the researchers at JCU using a combination of fun media tools such as Twitter.

What is your favourite animal? I'm a real nature lover, so this is a hard question for me to answer. My personal favorite is the New Zealand eagle ray.

What is the worst or hardest part of your job? Being a marine biologist is not all glamour, and sometimes getting into the water day after day even when it's cold, windy and wet outside can be challenging.

Knowing what you know now, what's one piece of advice you would give kids about the ocean? Let the ocean inspire you. There are many ways to do this: go for a swim, learn to snorkel or scuba dive; and if getting into the water is not your thing, then watch documentaries or read books that describe the beauty of marine life.

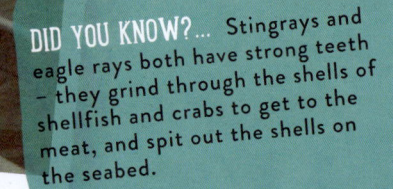

DID YOU KNOW?... Stingrays and eagle rays both have strong teeth – they grind through the shells of shellfish and crabs to get to the meat, and spit out the shells on the seabed.

DID YOU KNOW?... Eagle rays and stingrays are closely related to sharks, having skeletons made from cartilage — which is lighter and more flexible than bone — and a sandpaper-like skin.

WHAI / WHAI KEO
STINGRAYS / EAGLE RAYS

DASYATIS THETIDIS
MYLIOBATIS TENUICAUDATUS

DID YOU KNOW?... Females grow both faster and to a greater size than males. Their skin is 50% thicker than the male's, which provides protection during mating.

AOTEAROA – NEW ZEALAND WHANGATEAU

WHANGATEAU
OMAHA
X MY HOUSE!

LOVE YOUR OCEAN YOUNG OCEAN EXPLORERS

16

LOVE OUR OCEAN

YOUNG OCEAN EXPLORERS

WAHAPŪ
HARBOURS
BABY FISH PARADISE!

WAHAPŪ
HARBOURS
BABY FISH PARADISE!

"Have you ever thought about what it would be like to be a baby fish?"

Just imagine – you're only a few weeks old and you're floating around in a gigantic ocean where everything wants to eat you!

MAN, I'M GETTING FREAKED OUT JUST THINKING ABOUT IT!

I was stoked when Dad told me that we were heading to the Whangateau Harbour to go looking for baby fish. I've snorkelled there before and it's...

AWESOME!!!

Joining us on this cool adventure was one of Dad's good mates, Dr Tom Trnski, (a baby fish expert; he's even written books on them) and also one of my good little buddies, my baby brother Lucas. Well, Lucas isn't exactly a baby anymore - but he's still real cute and will always be my baby bro.

We headed to the harbour at high tide, which is when Dad reckons it's the best time to visit. He says this is when the water is clearest but when I asked him why, he told me to wait until we'd finished snorkelling and see if I could figure it out for myself!

HMMM, NOT SURE ABOUT THAT ONE...

You've grown 1mm today

DID YOU KNOW?... Baby fish like snapper and parore can grow 1mm a day in their first months of life.

DID YOU KNOW?... Pipis can filter at least one litre per hour each - that's a lot of water getting cleaned!

Baby Parore

Not as scary as I thought!

He sure was right about the water being clear at high tide though. As I stuck my head under the water it was like a busy city - there was heaps going on under there! Schools of baby parore were facing into the current, hovering above the fields of Neptune's Necklace seaweed and picking up little particles of food that drifted by. If we made any sudden movements they quickly darted away for cover and hid. They really were scared!

Dad started pointing at the sandy bottom and I couldn't make out what he was so excited about - it just looked like sand to me. But when we got closer, all of a sudden I could see tiny fish, about half the length of my little pinky. Man, they were hard to see - almost invisible! Their little tails kicked frantically, facing them into the current. Dr Trnski said they were tiny snapper that would have been less than a couple of months old.

Wow! Because they're so little they stick together in schools for protection against predators.

Down on the seabed were lots of crustaceans like shrimps, hermit crabs and mud crabs with eyes out on stalks. Dr Trnski even found a pipe fish which looked exactly like a little stick to me until he picked it up off the bottom and it moved its tail. Although we looked for flounder we didn't see any – Dad says they're so good at camouflaging against the sand that we may have swum right over them without noticing. The harbour seems to be a place where lots of things are good at hiding!

Dad told me about the way larger snapper, kingfish and kahawai regularly enter the harbour in search of food – including baby fish. Another freaky harbour predator is the John Dory. Known as a stealth hunter, this tall, thin fish waits quietly then surprises its prey by throwing out a huge mouth. Baby fish are in constant danger with all these predators about, and underwater plants are a life-saver for them. Mangrove forests, rushes and sea grass all make great hiding places.

Flounder

WAHAPŪ HARBOURS

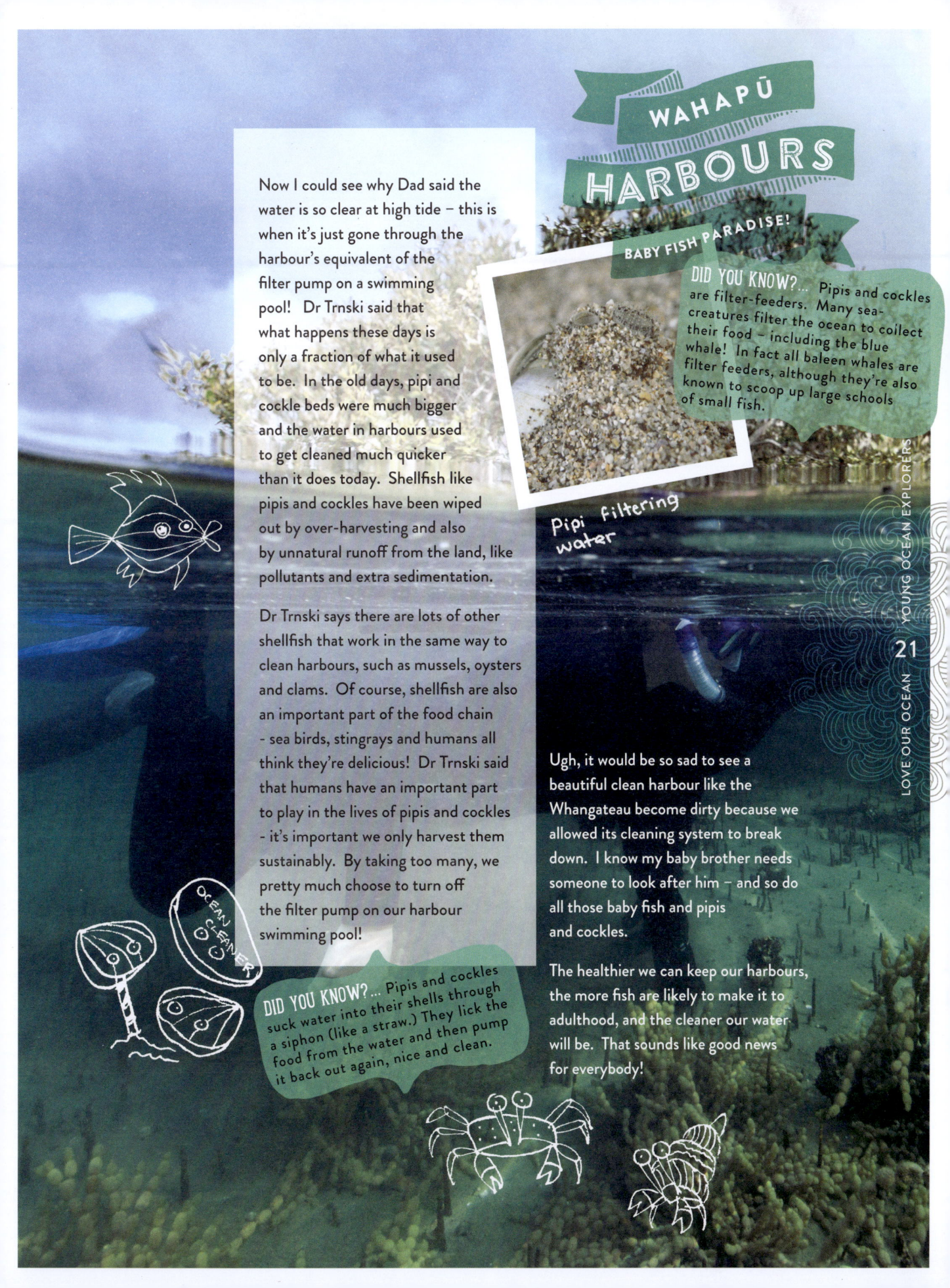

BABY FISH PARADISE!

Now I could see why Dad said the water is so clear at high tide – this is when it's just gone through the harbour's equivalent of the filter pump on a swimming pool! Dr Trnski said that what happens these days is only a fraction of what it used to be. In the old days, pipi and cockle beds were much bigger and the water in harbours used to get cleaned much quicker than it does today. Shellfish like pipis and cockles have been wiped out by over-harvesting and also by unnatural runoff from the land, like pollutants and extra sedimentation.

Dr Trnski says there are lots of other shellfish that work in the same way to clean harbours, such as mussels, oysters and clams. Of course, shellfish are also an important part of the food chain - sea birds, stingrays and humans all think they're delicious! Dr Trnski said that humans have an important part to play in the lives of pipis and cockles - it's important we only harvest them sustainably. By taking too many, we pretty much choose to turn off the filter pump on our harbour swimming pool!

DID YOU KNOW?... Pipis and cockles suck water into their shells through a siphon (like a straw.) They lick the food from the water and then pump it back out again, nice and clean.

DID YOU KNOW?... Pipis and cockles are filter-feeders. Many sea-creatures filter the ocean to collect their food – including the blue whale! In fact all baleen whales are filter feeders, although they're also known to scoop up large schools of small fish.

Pipi filtering water

Ugh, it would be so sad to see a beautiful clean harbour like the Whangateau become dirty because we allowed its cleaning system to break down. I know my baby brother needs someone to look after him – and so do all those baby fish and pipis and cockles.

The healthier we can keep our harbours, the more fish are likely to make it to adulthood, and the cleaner our water will be. That sounds like good news for everybody!

Meet the Gurus

HARBOUR GURU

TOM TRNSKI

Nationality? Australian.

Do you have any hobbies? Football, swimming, diving, listening to music. I love reading but don't have much time to do it. Being outdoors camping with a few friends and family is my idea of heaven.

Why did you decide to be a scientist? When at school I was good at maths and biology. I left school not sure what degree I was going to do. I tried civil engineering during work experience but it wasn't what I wanted to do. I wanted to be outside. I started a general science degree then I heard of a marine biology course and transferred to Townsville from Melbourne. This really opened my eyes to different environments. I loved being on boats and around the water – I realized this was what I wanted to do for the rest of my life. When I finished with a degree in marine biology there weren't many jobs. I volunteered in a museum for one day a week and was then offered three days work for six weeks, doing drawings of baby fish. This led to writing a book about larval fish which kick-started my career in marine biology.

How long have you been working in science? 30 years.

Where do you work? Auckland Museum.

When did you learn to swim? I was a very poor swimmer as a child, and still remember the scary experience of sinking to the sand at a Melbourne beach when playing with my father. It wasn't until I went to university that I spent time in a pool, swimming thousands of laps until I found a rhythm that suited me, and I built up my confidence in the water.

Knowing what you know now, what's one piece of advice you would give kids about the ocean? Learn to swim as soon as you can and become confident in the water. Most things in the sea are not dangerous - enquire about what you see and explore cautiously. As your knowledge grows, you will appreciate and understand the sea more.

One pipi can clean at least this much water every day

What do you think would happen to the harbour if we took all the pipis and cockles?

YOE

DID YOU KNOW?... Cockles inhabit tidal mudflats, but pipis are found in the sandier waters near harbour mouths where there is a strong water flow.

WAHA HARBOURS
BABY FISH PARADISE!

LOVE OUR OCEAN

YOUNG OCEAN EXPLORERS

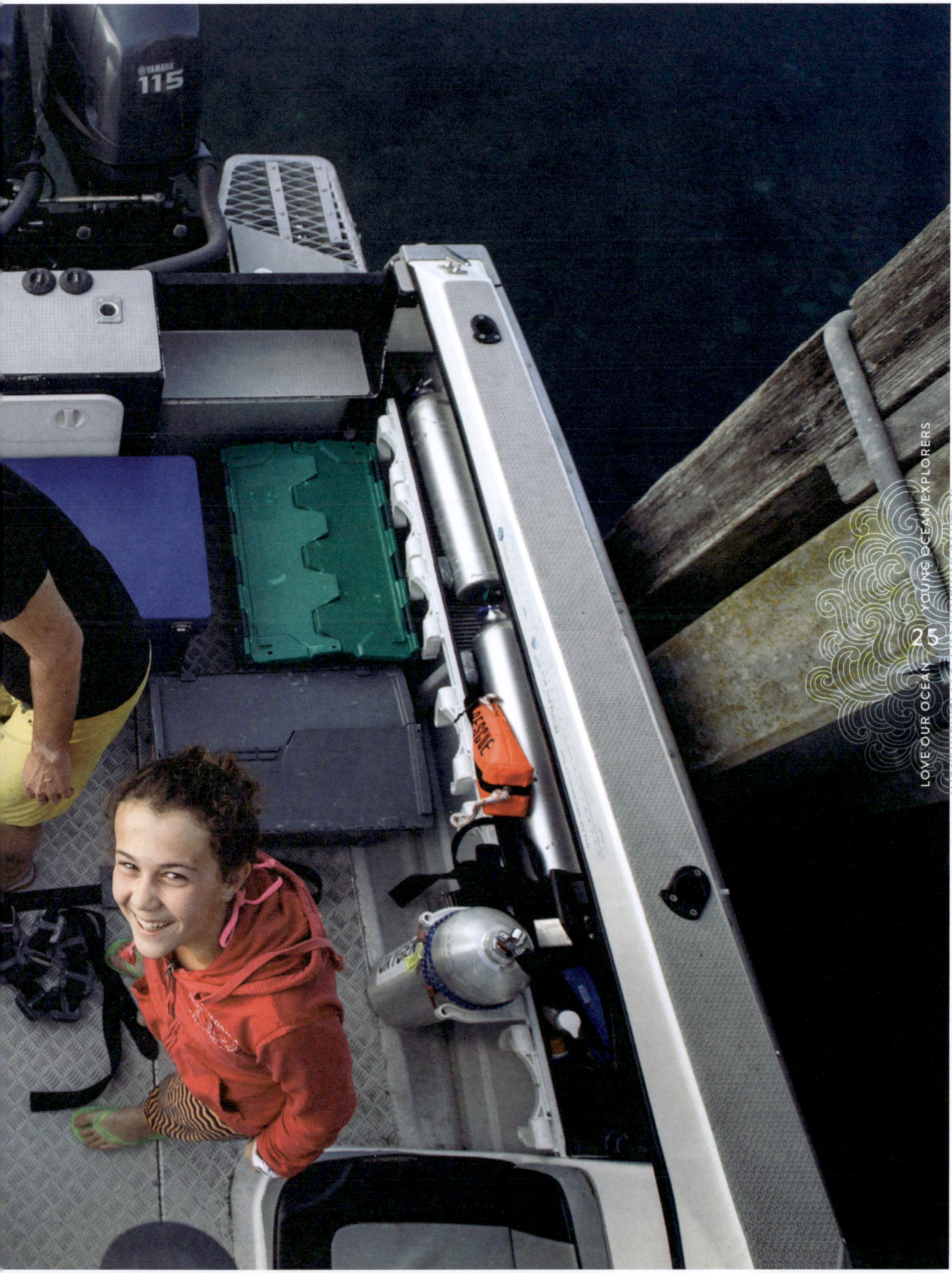

AOTEAROA ~ NEW ZEALAND GOAT ISLAND

GOAT ISLAND
LEIGH
OMAHA

26 LOVE OUR OCEAN YOUNG OCEAN EXPLORERS

LOVE OUR OCEAN

KOURA
CRAYFISH
JASUS EDWARDSII

KOURA
CRAYFISH
JASUS EDWARDSII

Haha – that's me

"Can you imagine being so delicious that everything wanted to eat you!"

That's the life of a crayfish. To protect that scrumptious flesh they walk around in a suit of armour – and hide away in caves during daylight hours!

Most things in the ocean would like to get their teeth into a crayfish and that includes two-legged visitors like my dad – he's been bringing crayfish home for as long as I can remember. Barbequed crays are pretty popular at our house!

I'm not sure if I'd like to be quite this popular, but one thing's for sure – if I had to be a crayfish I'd be praying really hard to get to live in a marine reserve, where crayfish are protected – at least from two-legged predators!

My baby bro Lucas ♥'s crayfish.

DID YOU KNOW?... In New Zealand crayfish are one of the predators that keep kina numbers in a healthy balance – if there are not enough predators, the kina numbers increase and they then eat down the kelp forests.

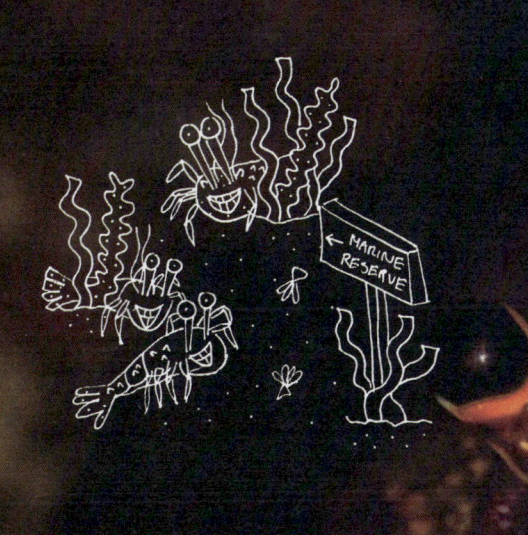

Their beady eyes creep me out!

DID YOU KNOW?... Female crayfish lay around half a million eggs, although only a few of these will reach adulthood.

Someone who really knows his crayfish is Dad's friend, Dr Roger Grace. He's one of the godfathers of marine conservation in New Zealand and he has seen a whole lot of changes in the crayfish world over the years. Dr Grace came with us to Goat Island Marine Reserve where there are heaps of crayfish today, but he told us that it hasn't always been this way.

Back when Goat Island Marine Reserve was first created, heavy fishing had left the crayfish population really small. Since then, numbers have quickly multiplied. Dr Grace has monitored crayfish numbers at nearby Tawharanui Marine Reserve for years. At the beginning there were hardly any, but now he's finding nearly 1,000 legal sized crayfish in a hectare of the reserve (a hectare is about the size of two football fields).

THAT'S AMAZING!

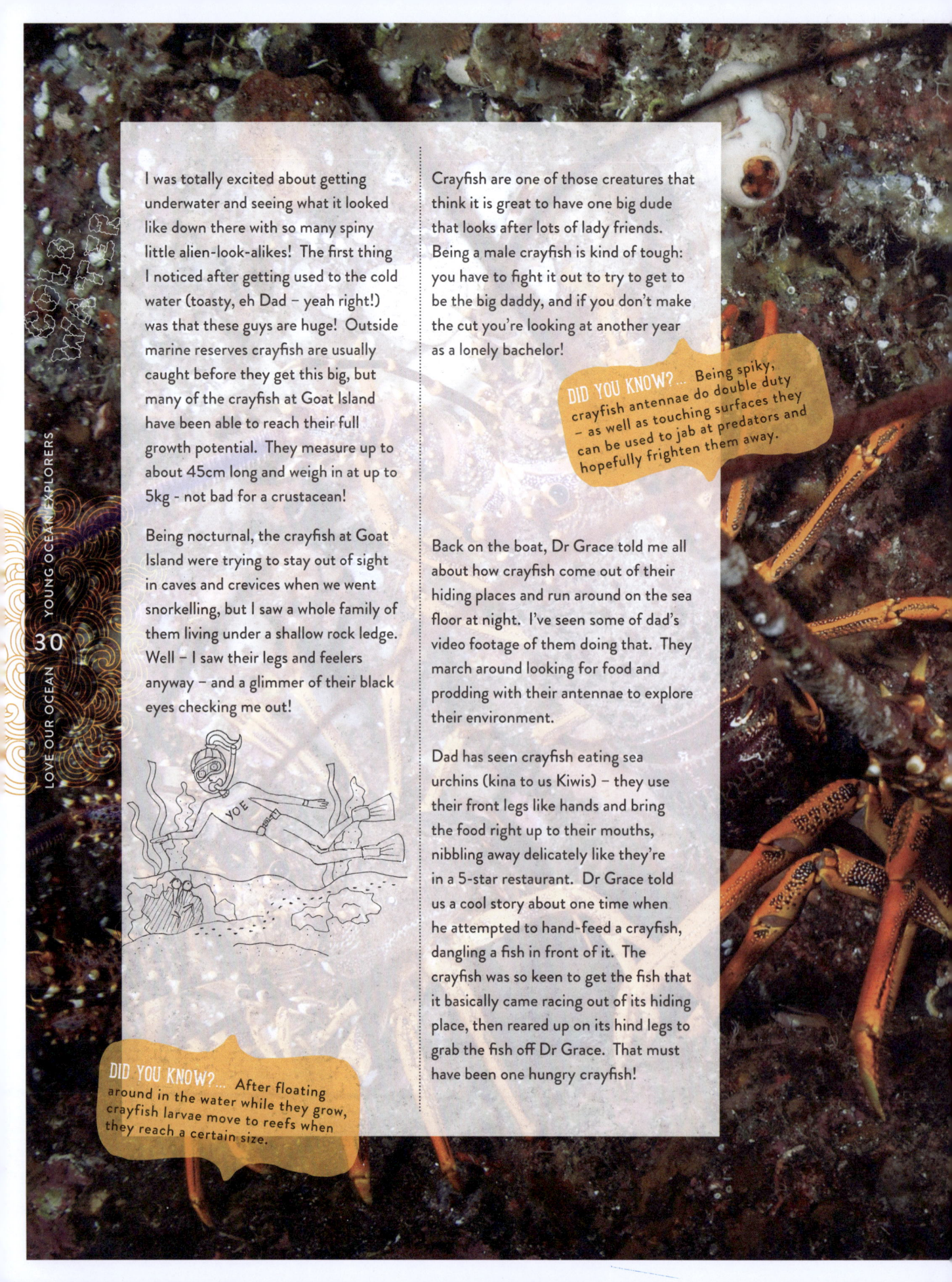

I was totally excited about getting underwater and seeing what it looked like down there with so many spiny little alien-look-alikes! The first thing I noticed after getting used to the cold water (toasty, eh Dad – yeah right!) was that these guys are huge! Outside marine reserves crayfish are usually caught before they get this big, but many of the crayfish at Goat Island have been able to reach their full growth potential. They measure up to about 45cm long and weigh in at up to 5kg - not bad for a crustacean!

Being nocturnal, the crayfish at Goat Island were trying to stay out of sight in caves and crevices when we went snorkelling, but I saw a whole family of them living under a shallow rock ledge. Well – I saw their legs and feelers anyway – and a glimmer of their black eyes checking me out!

Crayfish are one of those creatures that think it is great to have one big dude that looks after lots of lady friends. Being a male crayfish is kind of tough: you have to fight it out to try to get to be the big daddy, and if you don't make the cut you're looking at another year as a lonely bachelor!

DID YOU KNOW?... Being spiky, crayfish antennae do double duty – as well as touching surfaces they can be used to jab at predators and hopefully frighten them away.

Back on the boat, Dr Grace told me all about how crayfish come out of their hiding places and run around on the sea floor at night. I've seen some of dad's video footage of them doing that. They march around looking for food and prodding with their antennae to explore their environment.

Dad has seen crayfish eating sea urchins (kina to us Kiwis) – they use their front legs like hands and bring the food right up to their mouths, nibbling away delicately like they're in a 5-star restaurant. Dr Grace told us a cool story about one time when he attempted to hand-feed a crayfish, dangling a fish in front of it. The crayfish was so keen to get the fish that it basically came racing out of its hiding place, then reared up on its hind legs to grab the fish off Dr Grace. That must have been one hungry crayfish!

DID YOU KNOW?... After floating around in the water while they grow, crayfish larvae move to reefs when they reach a certain size.

Crayfish have the freakiest growth habit – because of having an exoskeleton (a hard outer body instead of bones to support their flesh), they can't just grow slowly like we do. They have to split out of their shell every year and let the softer shell underneath swell up and harden into a new, bigger shell. It's kind of like going up a shoe size each year. Crayfish are super-vulnerable while they're in between exoskeletons because they're almost like jelly when they shed their shell. It's at this time that they are most likely to be targeted by octopuses and moray eels – that sounds scary!

Scientists have discovered that crayfish make some really epic journeys. The eggs are laid in New Zealand waters but when the larvae hatch, they head to the warm waters of the South Pacific to do their growing. This journey alone takes them 1-2 years and once they're there, they drift around on ocean currents, growing and taking on different forms, before turning into miniature crayfish and heading back to the place they were born. How do they know how to navigate back across thousands of kilometres when they're only a couple of centimetres long? I don't know – and neither do scientists yet! It's one of the wonders and mysteries of the ocean.

DID YOU KNOW?... Female crayfish carry their eggs under their tails. When the eggs hatch, they release the larvae by lifting their tails and shaking them so that all the larvae drift into the water.

Crayfish are awesome and marine reserves are soooo helpful for replenishing their populations! It was so cool finding out what nature is capable of doing when it isn't under too much pressure – I can't wait to go back to Goat Island again!

Meet the Gurus

CRAYFISH GURU
DR ROGER GRACE

Nationality? Kiwi.

Favourite sport? Diving.

How has dive gear changed in your time? There didn't used to be wetsuits to keep you warm in the water, so we used to dive in woolen jumpers. Cameras have also changed, from film to digital.

Have your diving habits changed over time? I used to be really into spearfishing. In 1964 I came 4th in the National Spearfishing Championships. I gave up spearfishing in 1974 though, as by then I didn't like spearing reef fish and seeing the large numbers of reef fish that were killed for competitions. I came to feel it was a huge waste.

When did you get into photography? My Dad was a photographer. He gave me an old Practiflex SLR camera when I was 15 and we began building an underwater housing for it, but we were unable to complete it as Dad died when I was 16. My Mum put me through University and she bought me a Nikonos underwater camera for my 21st birthday. I invented a close-up rig for it and the success rate was very good, producing some amazing pictures for several years.

What kind of photography have you done over the years? I was a contract photographer for Greenpeace for 17 years, going on two major trips per year on ships like the Rainbow Warrior and Arctic Sunrise to shoot both underwater and topside photos. In 1990 I began photographing drift nets in the Tasman Sea. Working with Greenpeace took me all over the world – to Antarctica five times, the Indian Ocean, Canada, Scotland and the Mediterranean. I have also done some aerial photography, and writing and photography for local and overseas magazines including National Geographic.

Why did you decide to be a scientist? As a little kid I was always looking under rocks and looking in rock pools and was very interested in learning about marine life, so it was a natural progression.

Did you enjoy school and did you find learning easy? My experiences of school were variable, depending on the teachers. I was a pretty average student but I did have lots of opportunities.

DID YOU KNOW?... Crayfish have ten legs, two antennae and two smaller 'sniffer' antennae that they use to detect changes in the water. Wow – that's a lot of limbs!

KOURA
CRAYFISH
JASUS EDWARDSII

TODAY'S SPECIAL KINA

AOTEAROA - NEW ZEALAND

WHANGAREI

WHANGAREI

WHANGAREI HARBOUR

LOVE OUR OCEAN

YOUNG OCEAN EXPLORERS

MAKI

ORCA

ORCINUS ORCA

MAKI

ORCA
ORCINUS ORCA

"AN APEX PREDATOR that eats sharks for breakfast! ~ the loveliest animal on the planet?"

WHAT!?...
IS THAT EVEN POSSIBLE?

Well that's what dad's good friend Dr Ingrid Visser says – and she's the world expert! She's completely orca-crazy and she spends her whole life trying to help these black and white feeding machines. I've had a few encounters near orca; but one of my favourites was when an orca brought a stingray right up to our boat; it was like it wanted to show off its catch. They are so beautiful, and absolutely massive...

I LOVE ORCA!

I was so excited about going looking for orca with Dr Visser! We went to the Whangarei Harbour, to a sandbank where orca often hunt stingrays. While the rays are busy looking for crabs and shellfish, orca will cruise into the shallow water and try to nab them. If it's quick, a ray can try to dig into the sand and stay hidden, but once a ray has been spotted, a pod of orca will spend ages trying to nudge it out of the sand. When an orca gets its jaws onto one of those graceful wings, the ray is toast – orca toast that is. A second orca will come alongside and grab the ray's other wing. Then it's riiiiiiip...and snack time. Nice sharing guys.

Orca seem to know who Dr Ingrid is

Dad picking up orca leftovers... They dropped them in front of him

Dr Ingrid rescues a stranded orca

Male orca fins grow MASSIVE!

Hunting rays

Actually, the orca is kind of special in the animal kingdom because, just like human parents, orca mums teach their children about teamwork, cooperation and sharing. Hunting in groups gives orca a big advantage over ocean creatures that swim solo. A pod of orca will work together to surround larger prey such as a shark, bringing it to the surface where it is very difficult for the prey to escape.

DID YOU KNOW?... Orca have tummy buttons – in fact all cetaceans (whales, dolphins and porpoises) do!

Once the prey is surrounded, orca have a range of hunting techniques to choose from. They sometimes stun their prey by bashing their tail flukes onto it. Another method is for one orca to grab the prey and swim down. Held between the orca's sharp teeth, the prey finds it nearly impossible to break free, and eventually drowns.

Orca can hold on really tightly, even when their prey is thrashing and jerking. Their teeth are like a zipper, closing together perfectly; the top teeth fit down neatly into the gaps between the bottom teeth. No wonder these guys are at the top of the food chain!

Orca also communicate a lot when they hunt. They're like a sports team, calling out suggestions and encouragement. A particular click, call or whistle sends a message that the other orca in that pod can understand. It's all about family traditions; for a long time, orca have been working out how to hunt in their area and passing that knowledge on. In different parts of the world orca are taught local hunting techniques by their parents.

In Patagonia, Argentina, it's how to beach themselves briefly to grab a sea lion pup from the sand; in New Zealand, it's how to catch stingrays without getting poisoned by barbs; in Antarctica, it's how to wash a seal off an ice-floe.

DID YOU KNOW?... Orca like to move and they can travel up to 150km in a day. That's like going around a running track 375 times! Orca cruise at about 10km an hour, although when hunting, they can reach nearly 50km per hour.

37

DID YOU KNOW?... Baby orca are usually born tail first – unlike humans which come out head first.

I've actually seen orca working as a team. Once I went out on the water with my Dad and Dr Visser to rescue an orca that had her tail tangled in the rope of a crayfish pot. The other orca worked together trying to rescue her and pushed her to the surface so she could breathe. They kept coming up to our boat like they were asking for our help to free her!

As the rope was cut off the entangled orca, there were two others just under the surface next to the rescuers' hands, watching closely. It was like they knew we were helping them. This orca was so lucky and would have drowned if we didn't rescue her.

It was the best feeling to watch all six of the pod swim off together after being saved!

After that day I got a taste of how awesome Dr Visser's work must be.

Dad in his happy place

This orca kept coming up to Dad's camera for a look

DID YOU KNOW?... The word blubber comes from a Dutch word meaning to wobble!

38 LOVE OUR OCEAN · YOUNG OCEAN EXPLORERS

It's awesome watching orca from on top of Dad's boat

DID YOU KNOW?... Orca are true mammals – they give birth to live young, provide milk for their young, are warm-blooded, breathe air and are even hairy. Until it's six months old, a young orca has between six and ten whiskers on its upper lip.

Although orca have no natural predators, it's us humans that threaten them, with increasing pressure on ecosystems and their food supplies, and with pollution levels affecting water quality. Jet-skis and boat engines can also be disruptive and dangerous to orca. It's important to remember that we are visitors to their world, and to be respectful.

These beautiful creatures should be left alone for us to admire and enjoy.

ORCA ARE SO AMAZING!...
I hope you're lucky enough to see one in the wild one day!

MAKI ORCA
ORCINUS ORCA

SLOW DOWN

Meet the Gurus

ORCA GURU
DR INGRID VISSER

Nationality? Kiwi

Who do you work for?
Orca Research Trust (www.orcaresearch.org)

What did you want to do when you grew up? From about five or six years old all I wanted to do was work with orca. But I was told that the only way I could do that was to work at Seaworld. Even at that age I knew it was wrong to have orca in captivity, so I looked for a way to work with them in the wild.

Do you have any hobbies?
I love reading autobiographies and used to collect stamps, but now I only collect stamps that have orca on them.

Wow! so how long have you studied Orca for? Since 1992 officially, but I have absorbed every bit of information about them since I was a kid.

You must have been clever at school! I actually had real issues at school as I have dyslexia. I really struggled with spelling and maths.

You swim with Orca. You can't be scared of anything in the ocean!
Ha ha that's not true, I saw the movie Jaws as a kid and because of that I became terrified of sharks, but that doesn't keep me out of the ocean. In fact I'm now fascinated by sharks and swim with them as often as I can.

Has anyone inspired you? Three women scientists: Dr Diane Fossey (gorillas), Dr Jane Goodall (chimpanzees) and Dr Biruté Galdikas (orangutans). They respected the animals they studied and were willing to work with them in the wild.

What's the best and most satisfying part of your job? Getting to rescue orca and other cetaceans that have become stranded on the beach and to see the public become more aware and more caring about orca because of my research.

What's the worst part of your job? There is no worst part, but the hardest part is the constant struggle to find funding to keep the Trust going and to continue to research orca.

What do you want to achieve? I want to see better protection for animals in their natural habitat and no more orca in captivity.

DID YOU KNOW?... New Zealand orca are unique in that they eat a lot of sharks and stingrays. Scientists call this 'specialising' in a particular food. Antarctic orca eat lots of seals and penguins.

MAKI
ORCA
ORCINUS ORCA

DID YOU KNOW?... Eye patches on Orca are like finger prints – each one is different.

HAURAKI GULF

AOTEAROA – NEW ZEALAND

MOKOHINAU ISLANDS

AUCKLAND

LOVE OUR OCEAN · YOUNG OCEAN EXPLORERS

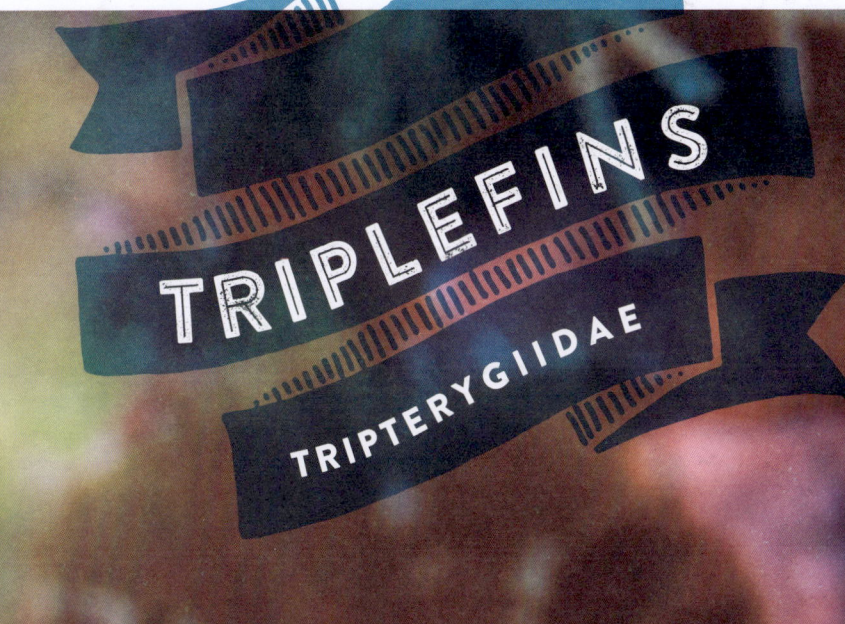

TRIPLEFINS
TRIPTERYGIIDAE

LOVE OUR OCEAN

YOUNG OCEAN EXPLORERS

43

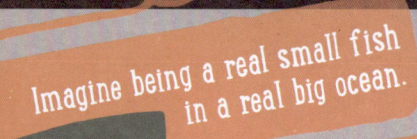

TRIPLEFINS

TRIPTERYGIIDAE

Imagine being a real small fish in a real big ocean.

IT'D BE FREAKY!

Especially if you couldn't swim very well and could only bounce around on the seabed.

You'd probably keep a pretty low profile, which is just what a cool little fish called the triplefin has done to survive in their fish-eat-fish world. In fact, they've done more than survive. There are over 130 species of triplefins found throughout the world and they don't seem picky about what temperature they live in – some are found in the tropics, right through to cooler waters. There's even one species found in Antarctica! The weird thing is – hardly anyone has heard of them!

Triplefins can be really different – I reckon that if you got these guys together for a family photo they'd look pretty funny. They come in all different sizes, colours and markings. One thing's for sure though – for a little fish, the triplefin has a whole lot of attitude!

What a hardcase looking family

My dad is crazy about triplefins. Actually, Dad can get a little bit too excited when he starts talking about them and it can be hard to get him to stop. You can imagine that I got a bit nervous when we met up with Dad's friend Adam Smith at the Mokohinau Islands in the Hauraki Gulf. Mr Smith is a triplefin expert. Would they ever stop talking so that we could get into the water and actually see some triplefins?

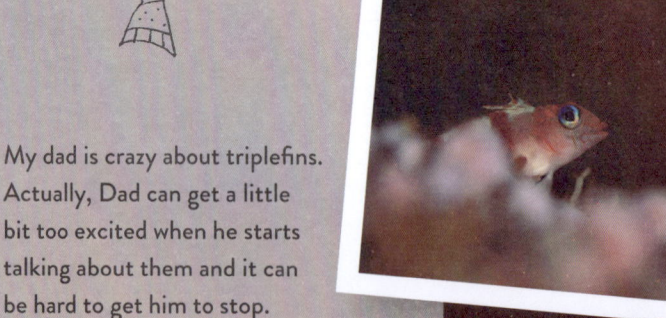

Blue-eyed

Yellow-Black

DID YOU KNOW?... Triplefins are named for the three dorsal fins that stick up on their backs.

LOVE OUR OCEAN | YOUNG OCEAN EXPLORERS

44

Oblique triplefin

Banded

Common

The only kiwi species that swims

Luckily for me, we finally went snorkelling and it wasn't long before we started seeing triplefins – once I got my eye in, we were seeing them everywhere. I hate to admit that Dad was right, but it was totally awesome seeing these cute little fish up close. Some of them seemed really curious – when I held my hand out very still on a rock, one fish even came right up to the tip of my finger. It was crazy looking right at this tiny little fish, with big intelligent eyes peering straight back. It seemed to be as interested in me as I was in it! Its whole body was shorter than my finger. My dad reckons that when a triplefin comes up to check out a human, it would be the same as me walking up to a creature as tall as the Eiffel Tower...

I'M NOT SURE IF THAT'S BRAVE OR JUST CRAZY!

One thing you notice straightaway about triplefins is that they don't really swim – they mostly sit quietly on the seabed, or on rocks and boulders, twitching their fins and swivelling their big, expressive eyes as they check out the scene around them. They are always on the lookout for danger and, because they're scrappy little fish, they're always ready for a fight!

Always keeping an eye out for danger

DID YOU KNOW?... Triplefins are carnivorous and mostly eat small crabs and crustaceans. Some have been observed cleaning the parasites off moray eels!

45

LOVE OUR OCEAN | YOUNG OCEAN EXPLORERS

DID YOU KNOW?... In some of the inner fiords of Fiordland in the South Island of New Zealand, triplefins can be found in really high densities. Sometimes there can be hundreds in a square metre.

When triplefins want to move, they propel themselves upward in a short burst of motion, before landing on the seabed again. Sometimes they flick their body to turn around and sometimes they hop straight forward. Triplefins hang out on the bottom like this because they don't have a swim bladder – something that keeps most fish species from sinking when they stop swimming. To get by without a swim bladder, triplefins spend most of their lives resting on their pelvic and pectoral fins.

Triplefins are territorial and will defend their territory against other triplefins. They're also ferocious when it comes to guarding their offspring from predators such as other triplefins and the sandagers wrasse, a reef fish which thinks triplefin eggs are extremely yummy. After the female triplefin has laid her eggs on a rock, she goes off to relax and the male takes charge of defending the eggs. He puts on a special 'guard' uniform – his colour changes to become brighter – and he'll even charge up to a large fish if he thinks it's coming to get his eggs...

THAT'S SO BRAVE!

Yaldwyn's

Blue-eyed

Cryptic

TRIPLEFINS
TRIPTERYGIIDAE

Scaly-head

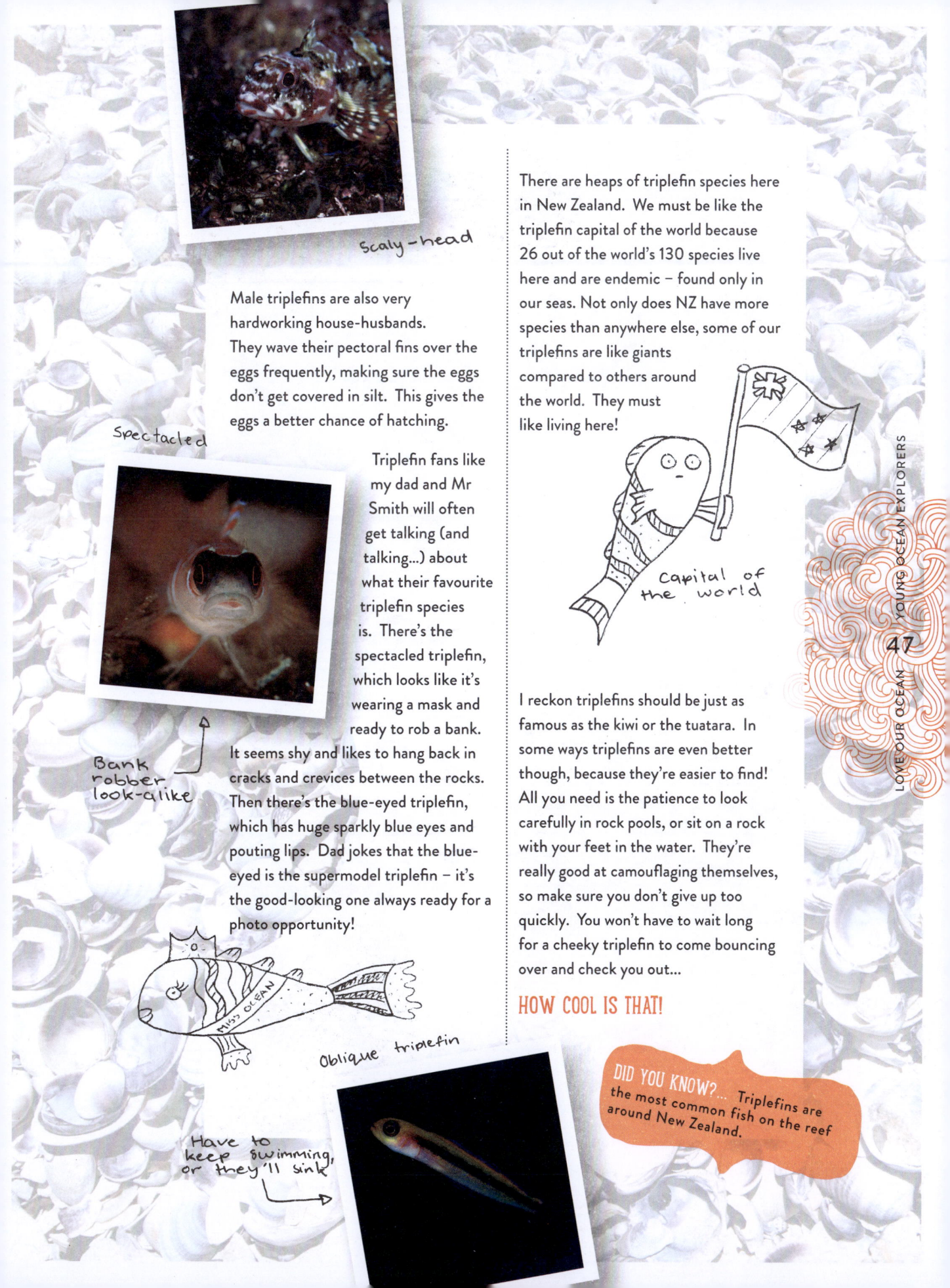

Male triplefins are also very hardworking house-husbands. They wave their pectoral fins over the eggs frequently, making sure the eggs don't get covered in silt. This gives the eggs a better chance of hatching.

Spectacled

Triplefin fans like my dad and Mr Smith will often get talking (and talking...) about what their favourite triplefin species is. There's the spectacled triplefin, which looks like it's wearing a mask and ready to rob a bank. It seems shy and likes to hang back in cracks and crevices between the rocks. Then there's the blue-eyed triplefin, which has huge sparkly blue eyes and pouting lips. Dad jokes that the blue-eyed is the supermodel triplefin – it's the good-looking one always ready for a photo opportunity!

Bank robber look-alike

Oblique triplefin

Have to keep swimming or they'll sink

There are heaps of triplefin species here in New Zealand. We must be like the triplefin capital of the world because 26 out of the world's 130 species live here and are endemic – found only in our seas. Not only does NZ have more species than anywhere else, some of our triplefins are like giants compared to others around the world. They must like living here!

capital of the world

I reckon triplefins should be just as famous as the kiwi or the tuatara. In some ways triplefins are even better though, because they're easier to find! All you need is the patience to look carefully in rock pools, or sit on a rock with your feet in the water. They're really good at camouflaging themselves, so make sure you don't give up too quickly. You won't have to wait long for a cheeky triplefin to come bouncing over and check you out...

HOW COOL IS THAT!

DID YOU KNOW?... Triplefins are the most common fish on the reef around New Zealand.

Meet the Gurus

TRIPLEFIN GURU ›

ADAM SMITH

Nationality? Kiwi

Do you have any hobbies? Scuba diving, snorkelling, playing outside with my kids (especially at the beach), tramping, travel, football, music, movies, and my beloved espresso machine.

Why did you decide to be a scientist? When I was at primary school, my class went on a tour of Canterbury University, which was right next door. The zoology department was wonderful—full of animal skeletons, fancy microscopes, even live spiders in glass cages. I made up my mind to study zoology that very day.

Did you enjoy school? I found maths and biology most interesting, so they were quite easy for me.

Where do you work? Institute of Natural and Mathematical Sciences, Massey University, Auckland.

What do you do? There are two main parts to my job—teaching university students and doing science. In my research I am interested in understanding why different species of fish live in different places. In a nutshell, I go and count fish and then analyse the numbers.

Are you scared of anything in the ocean? We're constantly told that the ocean is full of things that are out to get you, like sharks, stingrays, and jellyfish. In reality, this just isn't true. Humans kill around 100 million sharks a year worldwide. That's three every second! Sharks kill only around four people per year, so they have much more reason to be scared than we do.

A great white shark swam right past me once while I was scuba diving and I still have all my limbs! That day I saw for myself that they aren't as aggressive as everyone makes out. He probably just came to see what all the racket was about—scuba divers make lots of noisy bubbles! So, as crazy as it sounds, after seeing the world's scariest marine predator underwater, just a few metres away from me, I'm actually less scared of sharks.

In general, you should be much more concerned about the dangers of bad weather and for general water safety than about the wildlife.

DID YOU KNOW?... There is another commonly sighted small fish called the blenny, which is often mistaken for a triplefin. The difference is in the dorsal fins – a triplefin always has three – and triplefins also have scales on their sides.

TRIPLEFINS

TRIPTERYGIIDAE

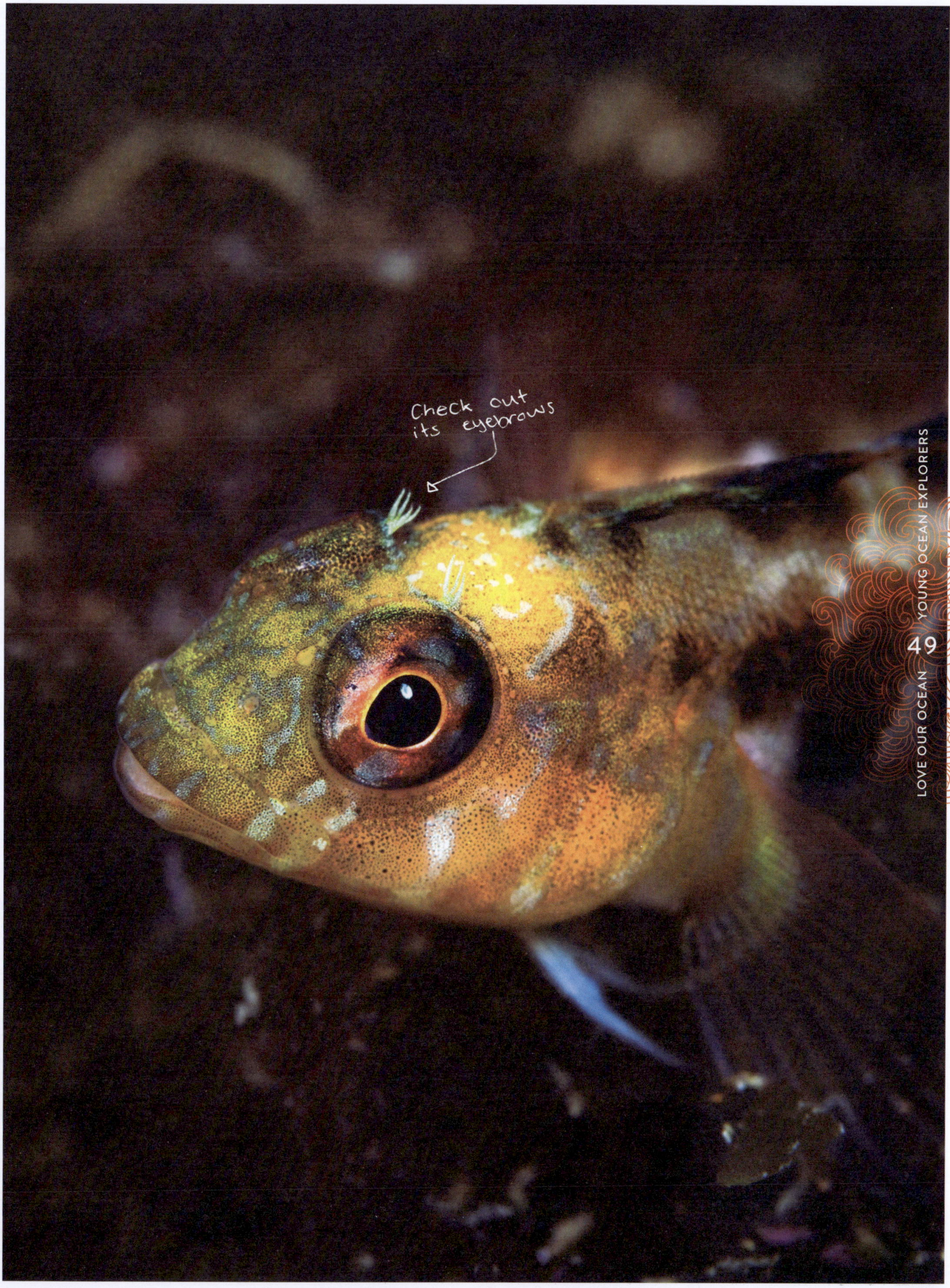
Check out
its eyebrows

BEHIND THE SCENES

YOUNG OCEAN EXPLORERS

I don't know about you, but I love seeing how things were made! We had SO much fun making the TV series of Young Ocean Explorers. There were some really cool and talented people making everything look good while the cameras were rolling! Here are some pics of what went on behind the scenes.

Cute bro Lucas

Good Morning TV show

Turtle release

LOVE OUR OCEAN

51

LOVE OUR OCEAN | YOUNG OCEAN EXPLORERS

AOTEAROA – NEW ZEALAND

WHANGAREI

WHANGAREI

HEN & CHICKEN ISLANDS

LOVE OUR OCEAN

YOUNG OCEAN EXPLORERS

SANDAGERS WRASSE

Coris sandeyeri

SANDAGERS WRASSE

CORIS SANDEYERI

"I knew there were some strange fish species out there, but this took me by surprise"

Male sandager

Off the coast of the upper North Island lives a colourful fish that sleeps under the sand at night. And – wait for it – while all of them are born as girls, later in life some of them transform into boys. Sounds like some kind of cartoon about a fish with super-powers, right?! And what I want to know is – how come I've never even heard of this crazy fish until now?

DID YOU KNOW?... There's over 600 species of wrasse worldwide and over 225 of them can be found in Australia!

My dad's friend and marine expert, Mr Wade Doak, knows all there is about life under the sea. He was happy to help us find out more about this strange fish with a strange name: the Sandager's wrasse. We skyped Mr Doak from the Hen and Chicken Islands. First of all I wanted to get to the question about all that weird girl boy stuff and why some girl sandagers turn into boys. Wouldn't it make things like having babies kind of... complicated?

...AND WHAT'S WRONG WITH BEING A GIRL ANYWAY?

Mr Doak reckons it's all about the way that sandagers have worked out how to survive effectively. Sandagers live in groups where one lucky male takes care of a harem of females. The male is the pretty one with a turquoise throat and flashy yellow, purple, black and white stripes on his sides. Living in a harem works well for sandagers, until disaster strikes and the male dies. Instead of waiting around to see if another guy turns up, the girls take immediate action. Within about two weeks, the biggest, bossiest one among them has turned into a male.

NOW THAT'S...
GIRL POWER

DID YOU KNOW?... The sandagers wrasse was named by Mr Sandager, a lighthouse keeper at the Mokohinau Islands. At the time he named the fish it was not known that sandagers wrasse tucked themselves into 'bed' under the sand each night. The 'sand' in their name is just a coincidence!

I even got to touch him!

Female

Having started to learn about sandagers, I was dying to get in the water and check one out for myself. Sandagers are known for being really tame and friendly – they seem to like it when humans visit their world.

DID YOU KNOW?... Sandagers eat small animals on the reef and they also love eating the eggs of other reef species of fish such as demoiselles and triplefins.

Dad said they're such friendly fish that they would even feed out of our hands. I was keen to try this, but to be on the safe side I wore a glove, which was just as well because one bit my finger. It was so amazing to be able to touch wild fish as if they were pets; one even swam right into Dad's mask. Watching the sandagers swim was quite funny. They are a demersal species – that means they tend to hang out close to the bottom. They rely on their pectoral fins to move around in a slow sculling motion most of the time. Only when they're in a hurry do they use their tail to propel themselves forward.

DID YOU KNOW?... In Fiordland, a cousin of the sandagers wrasse (called the girdled wrasse) is known for nipping divers on the lips.

Male

Dad has lots of cool diving stories and one of them is about the time he hung around to see a family of sandagers go to sleep for the night. Sandagers have the cutest habit of tucking themselves into bed at night. Hardly anybody has ever seen this happen and dad wanted to see it for himself, so one night he lay deadly still on the surface of the water, freezing his butt off for forty five minutes while he watched a family of sandagers. Just after dusk they started rubbing into the sand with their sides. Quickly, after checking they seemed safe, one by one they flicked themselves under the sand. The male waited to make sure his girls were safe before turning in...

HOW SWEET!

SANDAGERS WRASSE
CORIS SANDEYERI

Juvenile sandagers start off life as 'cleaner fish.' This means they spend their days swimming right up to larger fish and eating parasites off them – sounds yuck to me, but they're obviously yummy for the juvenile wrasse! The bigger fish don't mind, in fact they love it. For a fish, it's like having their daily shower! Larger fish will even hold their mouths open for a wrasse to swim in and clean around their sharp teeth . . . now that's a different way to get your teeth cleaned. Dad says you can sometimes see schools of fish chasing around a juvenile wrasse, all trying to get its attention so they can have their turn at getting cleaned.

In New Zealand there have been about 26 species of wrasses documented, but around the world there are over 600 species. The largest is the humphead wrasse which can grow to over 2 metres long and weigh over 190 kg. Wow, that's over twice as heavy as my dad. I'd love to see one of these someday, but there's no way I'll try handfeeding it!

What an amazing life story. Beds in the sand, harems, sex changes and staring your enemies in the face – I would never have expected so much drama from such a cute, friendly little reef fish!

THE UNDERWATER WORLD IS SO FULL OF SURPRISES!

Meet the Gurus

SANDAGERS GURU
WADE DOAK

Nationality? New Zealander

How did you get into diving? While I was at school I spent all the time I could finding ways to get into the water. We lived some distance from the coast so my friends and I swam a lot at the local pool. I quickly figured out that I preferred exploring the bottom of the pool, rather than splashing around on the surface.

Is it true that you invented your own diving gear as a kid? My family didn't have any money for diving equipment so I had to make my own. At intermediate school I made my own diving helmet from an ice-cream can. Two girlfriends took turns to pump air to me through a garden hose, from my dad's car tyre pump. With this gear we could dive to about six metres. On one occasion I found an old chalice (a ceremonial cup) in Lyttleton Harbour. At high school I made my own scuba regulator. I was caned in history class for working on it under my desk at the rear of the room.

Did you really find treasure on a shipwreck? In 1969 I was diving on the wreck of The Elingamite at the Three Kings Islands with Kelly Tarlton and found a stash of coins. I used the money from this treasure to start publishing books about the ocean. I've published over 20 books now including some for children, such as 'I Am a Starfish' and 'I Am a Fish Too'.

Who has been an inspiration to you? I was once invited to meet Jacques Cousteau (the world's most famous underwater explorer) at the Beehive table of our NZ prime minister. He has inspired my entire life. He told us we divers were the aquanauts, responsible for care of the ocean. We are its eyes for humanity.

Learn more about Mr Doak's work at www.wadedoak.com

Mr Doak in an early wetsuit

Real treasure from a shipwreck

SANDAGERS WRASSE
CORIS SANDEYERI

DID YOU KNOW?... The most common wrasse in NZ is the Spotty (Paketi). It's found all around NZ. Spotties are often caught from wharves.

Mr Doak's first underwater camera. He used it to take photos for the NZ Dive magazine, he started as a teenager.

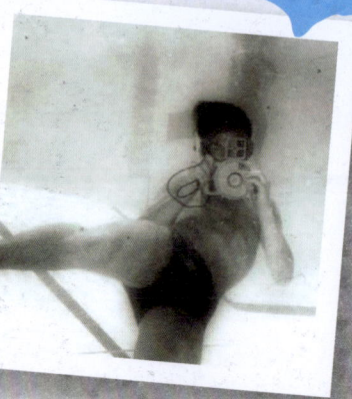

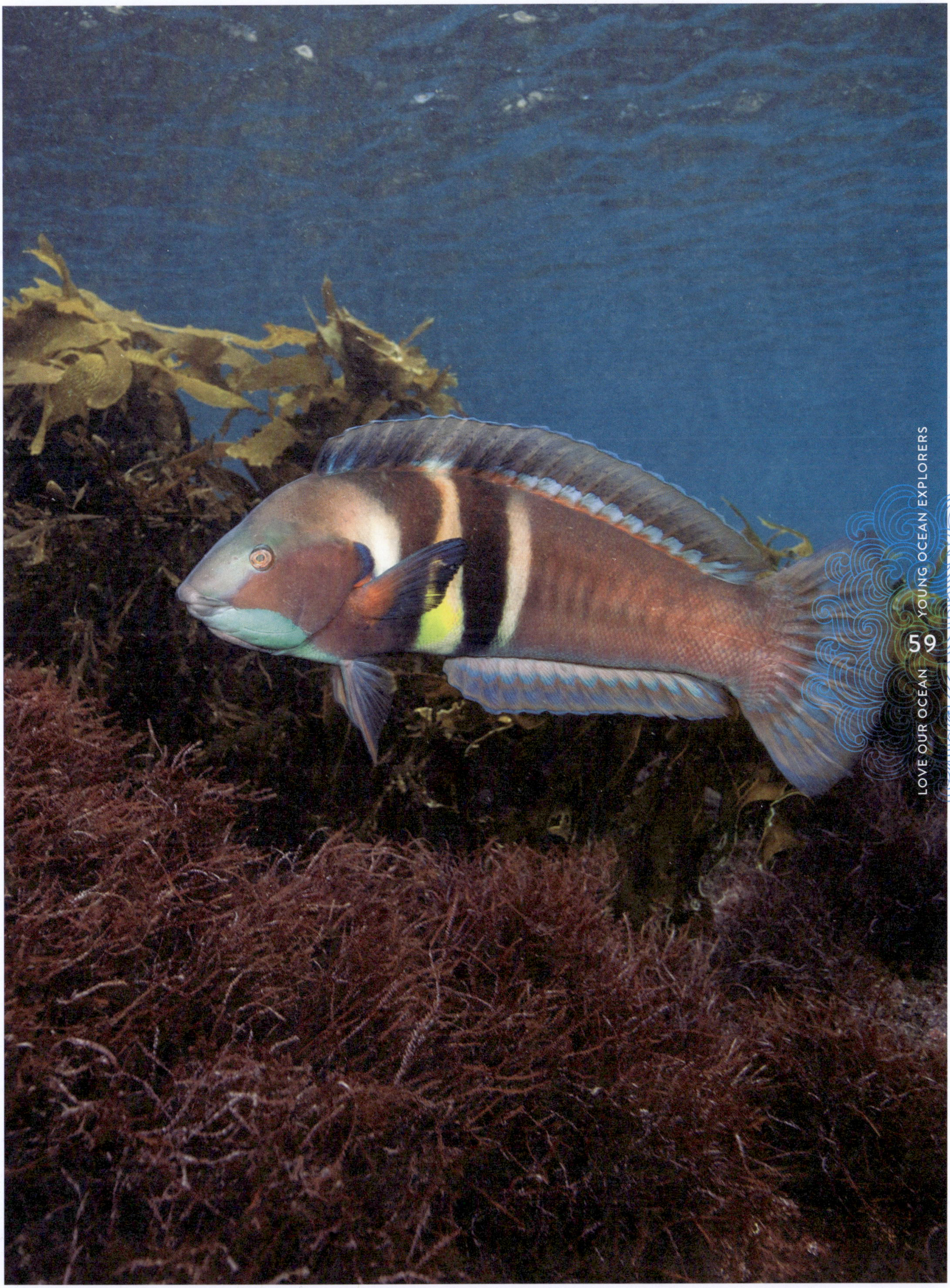

ABOUT my DAD

"My dad's life has always revolved around his love for the ocean and I get all my passion from him. I'll let him tell his story..."

Too cute Dad

I've always loved adventures. When I was growing up we made tree huts, raced down hills on home-made trolleys, headed to the local pond to catch tadpoles, and caught lizards for pets... but my all-time favourite thing to do was to go fishing – I couldn't get enough of it!

I remember as a kid reading the incredible fishing adventures of Zane Grey, a famous writer from the early 1900s. I was spell-bound, looking at the photos of his huuuuge fish caught in New Zealand waters... I truly thought he was the luckiest guy on the planet, and I couldn't imagine in a million years that I'd ever have adventures like his!

Fishing was my passion, but wearing a mask and snorkel in clear water for the first time was the most mind-blowing thing I'd ever done – beneath me forests of colourful seaweeds swayed in the gentle surge and a school of bright blue fish swam straight up to my face vying for my attention... from that moment on, another world opened up to me. I was no longer restricted with only trying to imagine what was happening under the surface... I was actually experiencing it for myself!

That's just weird Dad

60 LOVE OUR OCEAN YOUNG OCEAN EXPLORERS

Wow check out the hair

Bit by bit, as I got more comfortable in the ocean and my skills began to increase, my adventures grew as well. I now preferred to catch fish with a spear gun instead of a fishing rod... this led on to some amazing adventures, including pursuing big fish like marlin and giant tuna. I was now coming face to face with some of these huge creatures that I'd read about when I was a kid, experiencing something that was well beyond my wildest dreams.

Now, I get the biggest buzz when I'm capturing footage of this amazing underwater world so that I can share it with people like you. When I was a kid I could never have imagined that I'd get to experience anything like I have – swimming with marlin and sharks, filming orca feeding in front of me... some days it almost feels like I'm living in a dream. Capturing footage of the underwater world I love makes me feel so alive – it's like this is what I've been made for.

STEVE

LOVE OUR OCEAN | 62 | YOUNG OCEAN EXPLORERS

HAURAKI GULF
AOTEAROA – NEW ZEALAND
AUCKLAND

LOVE OUR OCEAN

YOUNG OCEAN EXPLORERS

AIHE

COMMON DOLPHINS

DELPHINUS DELPHIS

AIHE
COMMON DOLPHINS
DELPHINUS DELPHIS

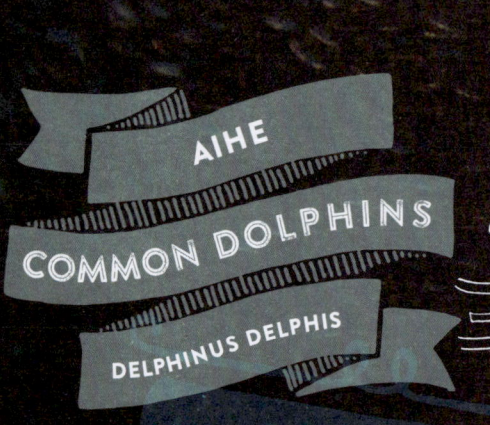

"Tall buildings, heavy traffic, lots of people and... DOLPHINS? WHAT THE HECK?"

Most of us would be surprised to know that there is an ocean highway right on the doorstep of Auckland, New Zealand's largest city. This highway is travelled by heaps of large marine animals including some of the friendliest in the world – dolphins! I absolutely love dolphins. They nearly always want to swim on the bow wave of our boat and they have to be the most amazing swimmers in the ocean – they make it look so easy!

We were searching for the dolphin species that is most common around the world – common dolphins. There are HEAPS of them in the Hauraki Gulf, but Dad had warned me that finding them might take some time. He said we'd need plenty of patience and good spotting skills; finding a pod of small dolphins in a big, blue ocean can be a bit like finding a needle in a haystack sometimes.

DID YOU KNOW?... All dolphins have conical teeth that are shaped like cones, with a point at the end. They allow dolphins to grip and then swallow their prey whole.

DID YOU KNOW?... All dolphins have only one blow hole, but some whales have two!

False killer whales are actually dolphins

DID YOU KNOW?... A dolphin's teeth emerge between three and five months of age, but unlike sharks, dolphins only have one set of teeth, which last a lifetime.

We had help from Dad's friend, Dr Karen Stockin – a common dolphin expert. I had heaps of questions about dolphins: for starters, I wanted to know more about a word I'd heard Dad use – cetacean. Dr Stockin said a cetacean is any type of whale, dolphin or porpoise, and that although we don't really get porpoises in New Zealand, we get heaps of whales and dolphins. There have been at least eighteen different types of cetaceans sighted in the Hauraki Gulf, and the most common of all is the common dolphin.

Like Dad said, though, common dolphins don't always seem that 'common' when you're looking for them! Hours of searching the horizon for little curved fins sounded like hard work to me, but Dad said the other clue would be if we saw flocks of birds diving into the sea. I've been out before with Dad and seen gannets diving into the sea like missiles. In the Hauraki Gulf, gannets and dolphins are sometimes found in the same feeding grounds since they both like to eat small school fish such as pilchards, jack mackerel and saury. (School fish are fish that stick together in groups, known as schools.)

I've seen plenty of Dad's footage of dolphins rounding up fish and it looks incredible; they work together to round the fish up into a tight ball. Sometimes they even blow bubbles in rings around the school fish to scare them even closer together. The fish move in unison like hundreds of silver spears as they frantically search for a way to escape, while dolphins swim circuits around them blocking their exits. Dolphins are incredibly fast and agile when they're hunting like this. Dad has the coolest story about how he's been in the water while dolphins were feeding, and the fish were actually hiding between his legs as they tried not to get eaten!

THAT MUST HAVE BEEN SO FREAKY!

We'd been looking for ages when Dad saw some small splashes in the distance – man, I was hoping this was finally going to be dolphins, as this was taking forever! As we got closer we could see that it was a small pod of about twenty dolphins ... **YAY!!** There were even some babies and juveniles (juveniles are pretty much teenage dolphins) – with the older ones.

I WAS SO EXCITED!

Dad slowed down the boat when we were a few hundred metres away, so we didn't scare them. Unfortunately, we weren't allowed to swim with them, which was sad – no one's allowed to swim with dolphins if there are babies with them.

AIHE
COMMON DOLPHINS
DELPHINUS DELPHIS

Bottlenose dolphins

Some came right alongside the boat and checked us out though – Dr Stockin reckoned they were just as interested in us as we were in them! Scientists have done lots of research into dolphin intelligence and it turns out that in relation to their body size, dolphins have the largest brain of any animal, next to humans. No wonder it feels like there's a special connection between us!

It's kind of hard to realise how much us humans have an impact on the dolphins in our 'backyard highway', but Dad said our rubbish really affects them.

Dad with the rope he cut off the dolphin

Once, he came across a dolphin that was tangled in a fishing line. It couldn't keep up with its pod as they fed! Dad jumped in the water with it and managed to cut the dolphin free, which is pretty cool – he said it was a very happy dolphin as it swam away and caught up with the pod again!

Dolphins are so much fun – we are so lucky to have them living close to us! Next time you're at the beach, spend some time looking out to sea... you never know when some of these friendly animals will be swimming past.

DID YOU KNOW? Dolphins may look as though they are smiling, but this is just the way their head is shaped – it is a design that makes them streamlined in the water.

Meet the Gurus

DOLPHIN GURU
DR KAREN STOCKIN

Nationality? Briwi! (British/Kiwi)

Do you have any hobbies? Walking my dog Macey, spending time with friends and family

Why did you decide to be a scientist? At the age of eleven I was keen to be a vet; however, after a stint of work experience I decided perhaps it was not for me. My passion for the marine environment really grew from there.

Did you enjoy school and did you find learning easy? I loved school but didn't always finding learning easy. In fact, I even retook my final school exams due to struggling under exam pressure and not getting the grades I really wanted. While I understood the work well, I had to work hard and it certainly never came easy like it does for some people. I don't think working hard to achieve something is always a bad thing though – it can make you want it even more.

Who do you work for? I work for Massey University, at the Auckland campus.

What does a normal day at work look like to you? Haha! One of the things I LOVE about my job is there is no NORMAL day!! Every day is different and I never know what may happen. Sometimes it's lecturing students, or writing papers on research. Other days I can be called to a whale stranding; be involved in health assessment of injured animals; go on road trips to recover dead marine mammals for examination or even undertake a post-mortem. No two days are ever the same and that is what makes my life so interesting!

What's your favourite marine animal? The blue whale, the biggest animal that's ever lived on planet Earth.

Are you scared of anything in the ocean and why? Absolutely - I have a phobia of multiple legs so anything with more than four legs starts to make me wince. As such, crabs, lobsters and crayfish especially freak me out!

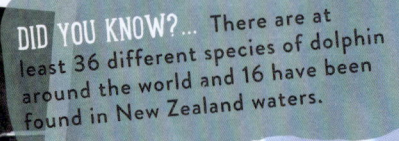

DID YOU KNOW?... There are at least 36 different species of dolphin around the world and 16 have been found in New Zealand waters.

AIHE

COMMON DOLPHINS

DELPHINUS DELPHIS

DID YOU KNOW?... Dolphins, like orca, have their babies tail first.

LOVE OUR OCEAN

YOUNG OCEAN EXPLORERS

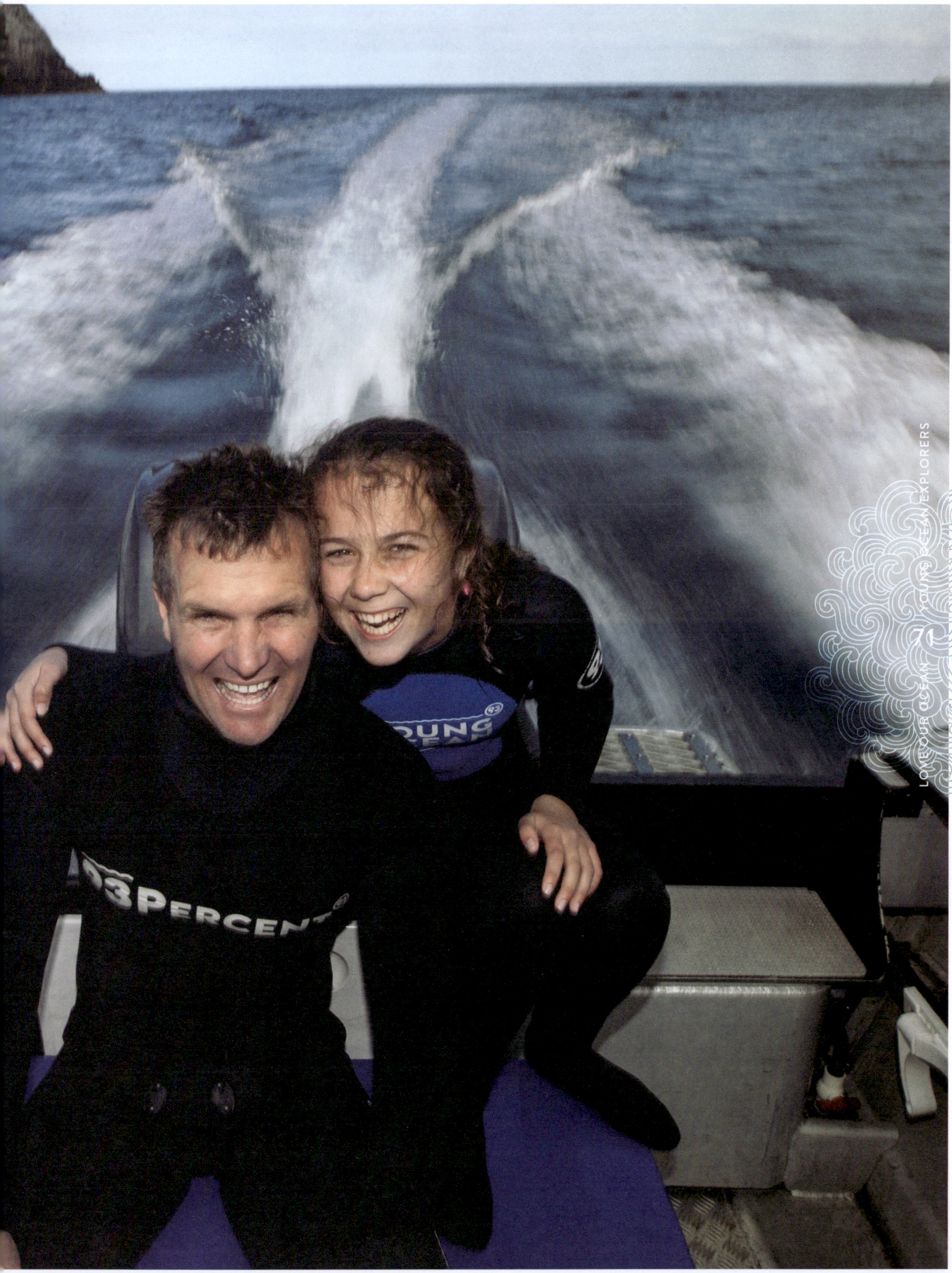
93PERCENT
YOUNG OCEAN

AOTEAROA - NEW ZEALAND
LEIGH

GOAT ISLAND
LEIGH
OMAHA

RIMURAPA
KELP
LAMINARIALES

RIMURAPA
KELP
LAMINARIALES

"CALL ME CRAZY... but when I go swimming, I don't like being tickled by mysterious slimy objects!"

So when Dad told me I'd need to sit in a forest of kelp for one of our stories I thought he must be joking. Not only is kelp slimy, but to me it looks like one big hiding place for my least favourite animal...

CRABS! YUCK. I DON'T KNOW WHY, BUT CRABS REALLY FREAK ME OUT!

DID YOU KNOW?... There are three main groups of seaweed: green, brown and red. Some of the larger brown seaweeds are known as kelp.

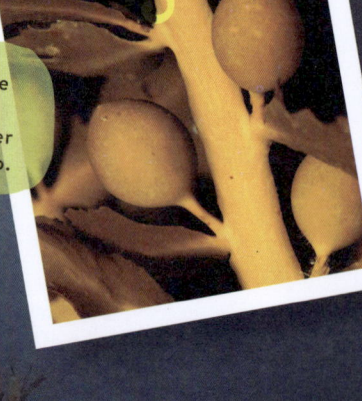

Even though Dad finally convinced me that no crabs were going to get me, I was still very nervous about sticking my head into the water with this thick carpet of kelp floating on the surface around me.

IT WAS HONESTLY SO SCARY!

Looking back I don't know how I got up the courage to do it, but I'm so glad I did. As soon as I peered down through the kelp I was transported to a beautiful new world. There was so much life down there. Although I really hate to admit this, my dad was right!

Getting through my fear was worth it. Instead of being freaky the kelp looked like a magical forest, swaying back and forward gently with the movement of the ocean. There were schools of tiny fish and shrimps hiding among the fronds. Dad was surprised and stoked that now it was me that was pointing things out to him — it was so amazing that I even totally forgot about the crabs!

DID YOU KNOW?... Seaweeds don't have roots like plants on the land; they absorb their food through their outside layers.

Dr Tim ripping it up

DID YOU KNOW?... Seaweed is a big algae (it's a macro algae.) The tiniest algae are called micro algae – they are better known as phytoplankton. They float in the ocean and are very important, as they're the start of the food chain and also provide a lot of the oxygen that we breathe.

Back on the beach after our snorkel we met Dad's friend Dr Tim Haggitt. Dr Haggitt is a marine scientist (although he looks more like a surfer to me!). He dives in seaweed beds all the time as part of his work counting marine animals for surveys, and he convinced me that kelp is way more interesting than just some random slimy sea plant.

Dr Haggitt said that in cooler, more temperate waters like New Zealand's, there is more food and nutrients for kelp to grow, so we have a lot of it. Cooler water is where most kelp forests are found. He explained that kelp forests create a healthy ecosystem, as many animals rely on kelp for food and it gives plenty of places for different creatures to live and hide: animals such as snails, fish, sponges and yes – crabs!

Dr Haggitt described how kelp survives in the ocean: it's really bendy and fitted out with flotation devices. Bull kelp has large honeycomb cells filled with air, so it bounces back from the waves and currents. Even the slime has its purpose – it helps kelp plants to survive when the tide goes out.

I was amazed to learn that there are at least 10,000 species of seaweeds worldwide. Some are tiny and others are massive.

GIANT KELP CAN GROW HALF A METRE IN A SINGLE DAY. THAT'S AMAZING! It adds to its own length faster than any living thing on earth! It can grow in water that is over 20m deep and when it reaches the surface it just keeps growing across the surface for an additional 20 or 30 metres. If you stretched out a single one of these gigantic plants it could be the length of a football field!

For something so vital to sea life, it was scary to learn that kelp forests can die out quickly. Sea urchins (kina) love eating kelp and if the predators that eat urchins are overfished urchin numbers may explode. At certain depths urchins can mow down a kelp forest.

DID YOU KNOW?... Some seaweeds are full of jelly-forming chemicals. When extracted, these can be used to thicken a range of products, from icecream to shampoo.

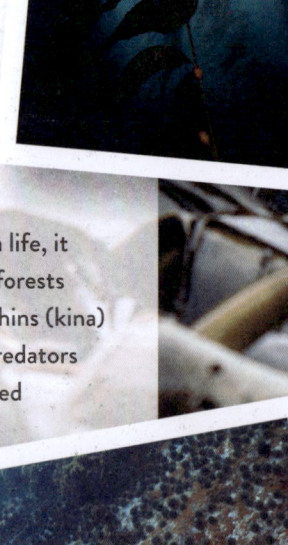

Kina Barron

Where I live, near the Hauraki Gulf, this is a problem. The main animals that eat sea urchins here are snapper and crayfish, and because snapper and crayfish are so tasty to humans, their numbers are down, meaning the urchin populations have exploded in places. Once the kelp is gone a range of species reliant on the kelp go too so only urchins are left on the sea bed. I'd much rather snorkel over a kelp bed full of fish than a whole lot of urchins!

So I've changed my mind. Kelp isn't that gross, it's beautiful. It may be slimy, but it's important for life above and below the surface.

I'LL NEVER LOOK AT KELP THE SAME AGAIN!

DID YOU KNOW?... There are at least 900 species of seaweed in NZ alone. About 1/3 of them are found only in our seas.

Red seaweed →

Hold fast

DID YOU KNOW?... Kelp needs light to photosynthesize just like plants on land do, so most seaweeds are found in less than 30 metres. Beyond that, there normally isn't enough light for it to survive. But some seaweed can live deeper underwater and one has been discovered in the clear waters of the Kermadec Islands in NZ, in water deeper than 200m.

RIMURAPA

KELP

LAMINARIALES

Meet the Gurus

KELP GURU >
DR TIM HAGGITT

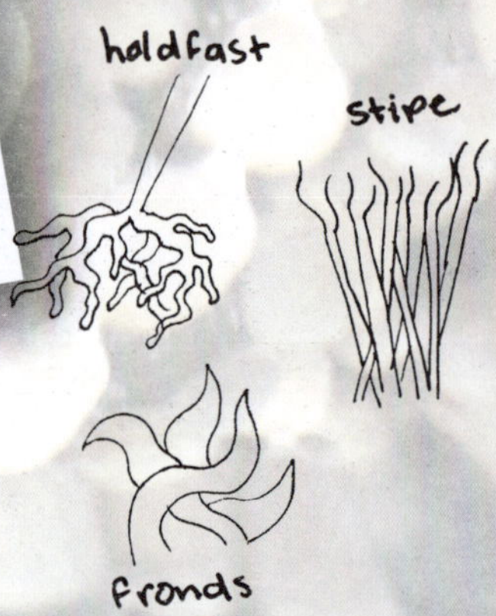

Nationality? New Zealand

Do you have any other interests? Punk rock music (loud and fast), spending time with the family and surfing

Why did you decide to be a scientist? At school I enjoyed carrying out experiments in science and trying to understand the secrets of the natural world.

Did you enjoy school... did you find learning easy? I enjoyed parts of school particularly biology and chemistry, but I was pretty rubbish at many subjects – particularly accounting. My hand writing was (and still is) terrible. I remember being the last in my primary school class to graduate from writing in pencil to pen (ha ha). It was not until going to University that it all started making sense and academically I started to do well.

What do you do? I study many aspects of seaweeds. We also undertake marine reserve surveys. These involve measuring and counting marine life on the bottom of the ocean for hours on end. Once the data is collected it needs to be analysed and then I write a report about it.

What does a normal day at work look like to you? Step 1: Strong coffee! Step 2: Check the weather and surf. Step 3: If not diving, report writing or some form of data analysis relating to current projects. Step 4: If diving, then a large part of the day will be underwater doing surveys – counting marine life on the bottom of the ocean - or experiments. Step 5: Try and get a surf in.

Are you scared of anything in the ocean? Octopus - because they're way smarter than I'll ever be and they enjoy stealing your pencil, datasheets and in some cases dive mask.

Knowing what you know now – what's one piece of advice you would give kids about the ocean? If you're passionate about the ocean, learn about it so we can work out ways together to use it sustainably and protect it; immerse yourself in it so you can always feel energised; respect it and everything that lives in it, so that we can use it and enjoy it forever.

holdfast
stipe
fronds

DID YOU KNOW?... In NZ, the main type of kelp that's traditionally been harvested and eaten is a smaller type of red seaweed called karengo. It's closely related to the nori seaweed from Japanese waters which is used to make sushi.

I LOVE SUSHI!!

RIMURAPA
KELP
LAMINARIALES

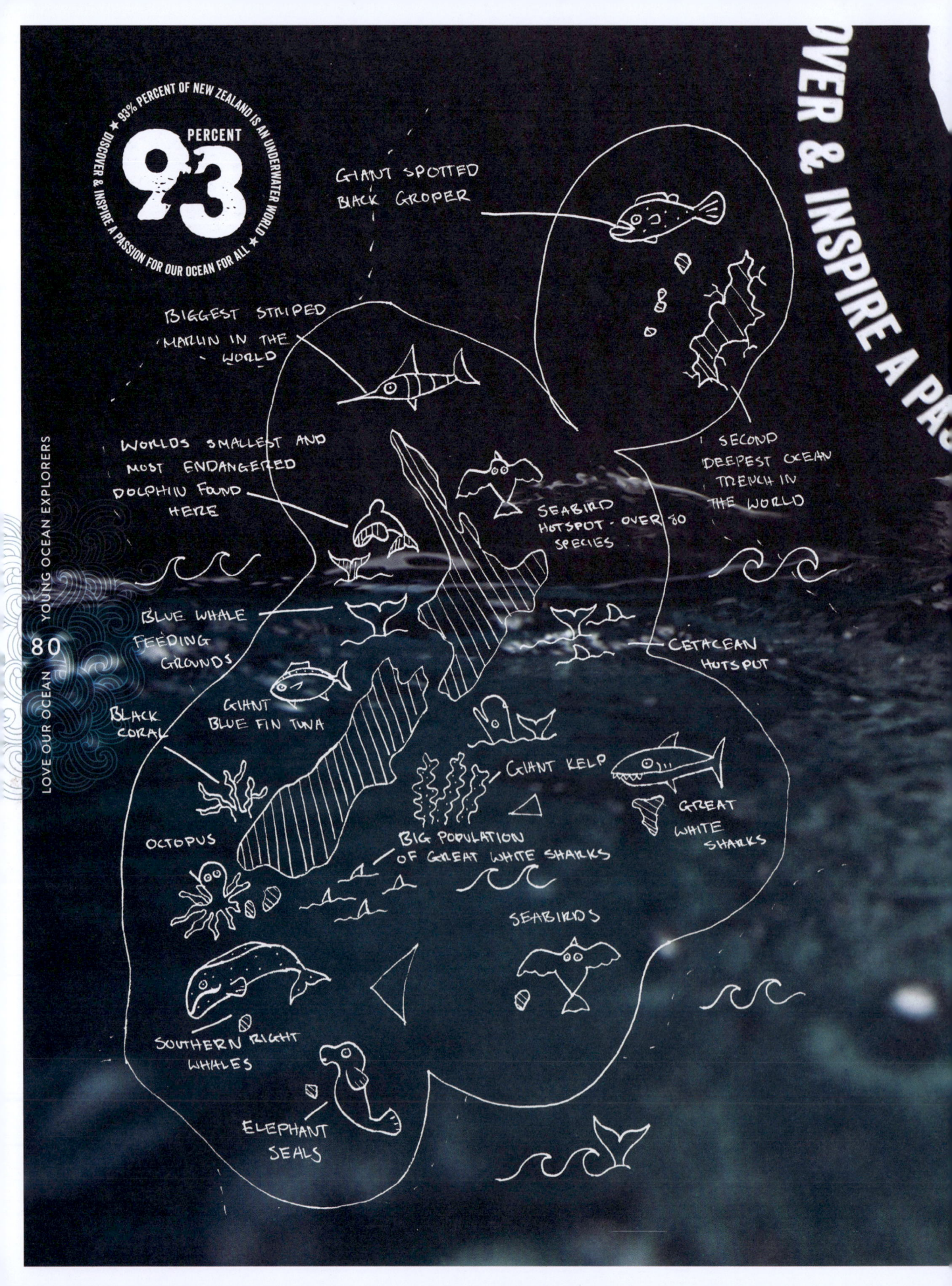

93 PERCENT — 93% PERCENT OF NEW ZEALAND IS AN UNDERWATER WORLD ★ DISCOVER & INSPIRE A PASSION FOR OUR OCEAN FOR ALL ★

DISCOVER & INSPIRE A PASSION

- GIANT SPOTTED BLACK GROPER
- BIGGEST STRIPED MARLIN IN THE WORLD
- WORLDS SMALLEST AND MOST ENDANGERED DOLPHIN FOUND HERE
- SEABIRD HOTSPOT - OVER 80 SPECIES
- SECOND DEEPEST OCEAN TRENCH IN THE WORLD
- BLUE WHALE FEEDING GROUNDS
- CETACEAN HOTSPOT
- BLACK CORAL
- GIANT BLUE FIN TUNA
- GIANT KELP
- OCTOPUS
- BIG POPULATION OF GREAT WHITE SHARKS
- GREAT WHITE SHARKS
- SEABIRDS
- SOUTHERN RIGHT WHALES
- ELEPHANT SEALS

YOUNG OCEAN EXPLORERS
LOVE OUR OCEAN
80

93

UNDERWATER WORLD
...FOR ALL ★

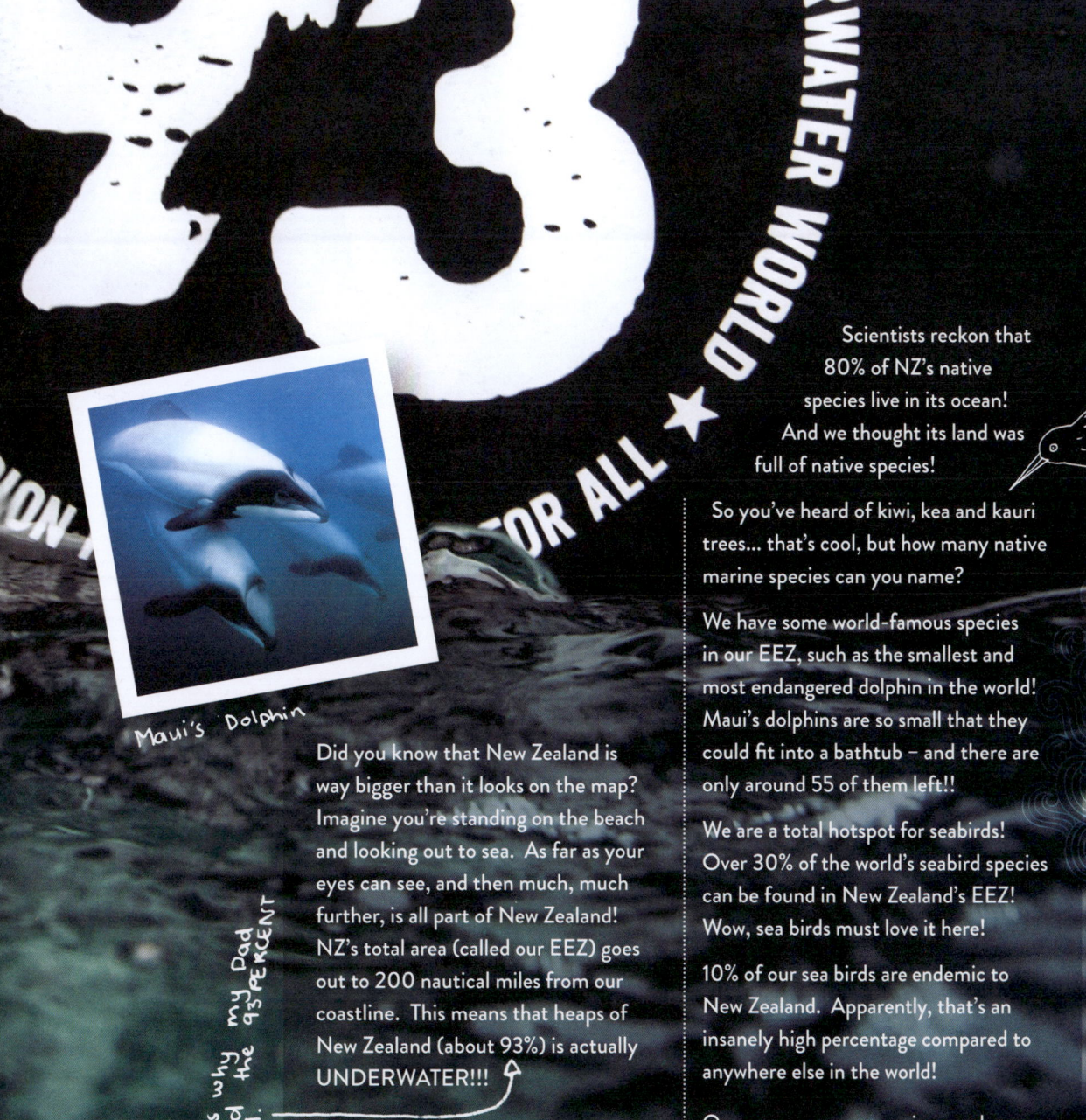

Maui's Dolphin

Did you know that New Zealand is way bigger than it looks on the map? Imagine you're standing on the beach and looking out to sea. As far as your eyes can see, and then much, much further, is all part of New Zealand! NZ's total area (called our EEZ) goes out to 200 nautical miles from our coastline. This means that heaps of New Zealand (about 93%) is actually UNDERWATER!!!

This is why my Dad created the 93 PERCENT brand.

In case you've never heard of an EEZ (I sure hadn't!), it means Exclusive Economic Zone. We have one of the biggest EEZs in the world! I think that's something to be proud of! It's definitely cool when it comes to exploring underwater.

Scientists reckon that 80% of NZ's native species live in its ocean! And we thought its land was full of native species!

So you've heard of kiwi, kea and kauri trees... that's cool, but how many native marine species can you name?

We have some world-famous species in our EEZ, such as the smallest and most endangered dolphin in the world! Maui's dolphins are so small that they could fit into a bathtub – and there are only around 55 of them left!!

We are a total hotspot for seabirds! Over 30% of the world's seabird species can be found in New Zealand's EEZ! Wow, sea birds must love it here!

10% of our sea birds are endemic to New Zealand. Apparently, that's an insanely high percentage compared to anywhere else in the world!

Our oceans are more unique and even more diverse than our land! Isn't it crazy that most of us don't know much about what's out there? And don't you reckon we should have a plan for looking after our oceans, just as much as we do for our land?

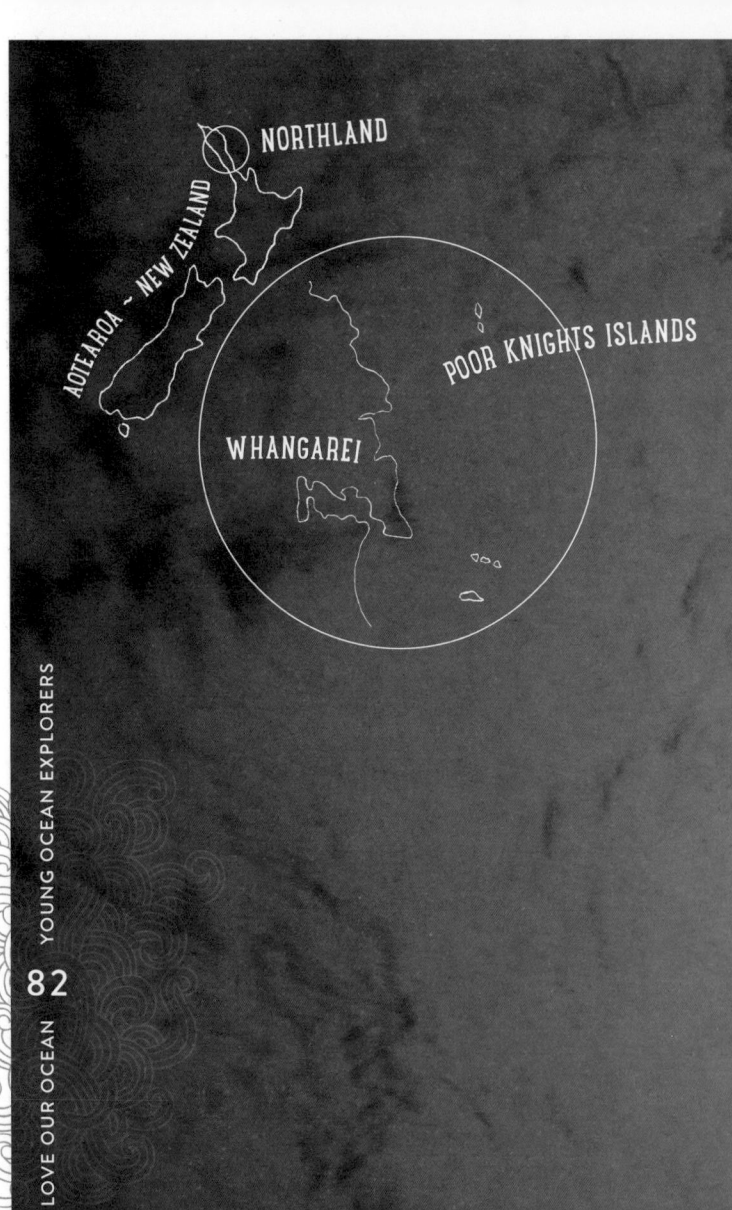

AOTEAROA - NEW ZEALAND
NORTHLAND
POOR KNIGHTS ISLANDS
WHANGAREI

HONU TURTLES

CHELONIOIDEA

LOVE OUR OCEAN

YOUNG OCEAN EXPLORERS

HONU
TURTLES
CHELONIOIDEA

Green turtle

"Whoa! ...a string of underwater volcanoes that have been carved by the ocean into caves."

That sounds completely amazing. Add to that, heaps and heaps of different plants and animals... and we were going to these islands to look for...

TURTLES???

Turtles are the coolest animals and they are not often seen in the wild in New Zealand. I was SO excited about this trip! The Poor Knights Islands are famous – they were named as one of the world's top ten dive spots, by one of the world's most famous ocean explorers (Jacques Cousteau). I've also seen heaps of amazing footage that Dad's filmed there. I couldn't wait to get into that incredibly blue water – it really is like paradise out there!

DID YOU KNOW?... There are five species of sea turtle found around New Zealand – the green turtle, leatherback, loggerhead, hawksbill and olive ridley. The green turtle is the most commonly sighted.

DUUUDE! SWEET!

As soon as we got in, we were surrounded by hundreds of fish. It was just how you imagine the ocean being before humans took too many fish – a wilderness humming with life!

There was one problem though. No matter how much we looked – no turtles! Dad didn't seem too bothered – he suggested we cruise around to the next bay. Anchored there was a huge boat with heaps of people on it! When I asked Dad what was going on, he said he just wanted to say hi to some friends on board the boat. I was nervous that he was going to talk for ages because he always talks too long! As we climbed aboard, I saw Dad's good friend, Dan Godoy, and a turtle sitting on the deck! WHAT?! Man, Dad is so sneaky – he knew all along... No wonder he was so sure we'd see a turtle!

I'd met Mr Godoy before when I did a school project about turtles and plastic. Mr Godoy is New Zealand's turtle expert, and Dad helped me to organise an interview with him as part of my project. Actually, that was the beginning of Young Ocean Explorers – seeing the interest of the students who viewed that project gave Dad the idea for our TV series.

On the boat there were also two kaumatua (elders) from Ngati Wai, the Māori iwi (tribe) linked with the Tutukaka Coast and the Poor Knights Islands. Then we met Stacey the green turtle – he was so beautiful! Stacey had washed up on a beach in bad condition. In New Zealand, turtles like Stacey are checked and given medical help at Auckland Zoo, before being transferred to Kelly Tarlton's Sealife Aquarium to be nursed back to health, so they can be released into the wild again. It often turns out that they have eaten plastic, which they can't digest.

That's so horrible! I can't believe that such a gorgeous animal should suffer because people are too lazy to put rubbish in bins properly, leaving plastic to blow around and end up in the ocean. I've seen footage of plastic floating in the ocean and it looks just like food that turtles would normally eat: a sponge, a jellyfish, or a nice piece of seaweed or algae. A turtle will gulp the plastic down and then it sits in their stomach, making them more and more unwell, and often getting joined by more plastic until the turtle dies. Mr Godoy told me about one turtle that died that had over 500 pieces of plastic in its stomach!

Plastic found in a turtles stomach

DID YOU KNOW?... Sea turtles feed in shallow harbours where rubbish tends to collect.

One thing ruined our feelings of happiness though. As we snorkelled back to the boat, enjoying all the amazing fish on the way, Dad and I picked up several pieces of plastic. These weren't bits of litter dropped by visitors to the Poor Knights – Dad said they would have drifted out from the mainland, which is at least 23km away!

DID YOU KNOW?... Leatherback turtles can travel huge distances. To go between their feeding and breeding grounds, they sometimes swim up to 6000km each way. That's like swimming from New Zealand to Mexico!

DID YOU KNOW?... Sea turtles aren't common in New Zealand; they prefer warmer waters – except for leatherbacks which have even been sighted in the Arctic!

Before we put Stacey in the water, I got the chance to see him close up and look at his amazing oval shell, curved flippers and round beaked face. We watched from the water while he was released: one of the kaumatua recited a karakia (prayer of blessing) and Stacey was gently placed into the sea. With a couple of quick flicks of his flippers he was free again. He looked so at home down there and it felt amazing to know he had a fresh start in life. A huge school of blue mao mao came and checked him out almost immediately. Stacey's new home looked so beautiful – if I was a turtle I'd love to live there!

Like Mr Godoy said – if every New Zealander picked up one piece of rubbish a day, that would be 4 million less pieces of rubbish to make it into the ocean – every day! What we do on land really does matter.

I love turtles!

MILLION PIECES

This definitely wasn't the turtle encounter I was hoping for when we set out on our adventure – but it was a completely amazing experience! I'm really glad I got to be part of something so special.

DID YOU KNOW?... Sea turtles are fully protected in New Zealand. If you find one on the beach call: **0800 DOC HOT**

GOOD LUCK OUT THERE STACEY!!

CALL 0800 DOC HOT

Meet the Gurus

TURTLE GURU

DAN GODOY

Nationality? NZ/Chilean (my friends call me a "Chiwi!")

Do you have any hobbies or other interests? Diving, Thai boxing, fishing, motorcycles, reading, movies, music, camping and tramping.

Why did you decide to be a scientist? I don't think I decided to be a scientist, it just happened. I was always curious as a kid so would always ask questions as to why and how things worked. I was especially amazed and inspired by nature so I guess those things combined led me to become a scientist.

Did you enjoy school and did you find learning easy? I enjoyed school because my friends were there but focusing and paying attention in class was hard for me. I was smart enough but I just spent too much time daydreaming about what lay beyond the classroom window. I think, like many boys, I learnt best by hands-on experiences.

Where do you work? Massey University. Sometimes I also work as a Dive Master and Scientific Research Diver.

What do you do? I study the biology of marine turtles in New Zealand.

What does a normal day at work look like to you? It depends on the task at hand. That's what is exciting about what I do, it can be so varied. One day I might be in the laboratory examining samples or writing up my research, while another day may see me out on the ocean searching for turtles.

What's your favourite animal? One of my favorite animals has to be marine turtles of course, but I also like manta rays, bees, mantis shrimps, bats, sharks, birds... too many to choose from!

Are you scared of anything in the ocean and why? Yes, pollution because of the damaging effect it has on marine life!

What's the best part of your job? Diving, and getting the chance to inspire school kids to make a positive difference in their world.

What's the worst or hardest part of your job? Sitting still at my computer for long hours trying to write my research I still get distracted easily!

When did you learn to swim or snorkel? I taught myself how to swim at the local pool when I was 14.

How many dives have you done? About 900.

DID YOU KNOW?... Turtles can hold their breath for up to several hours!

HONU

TURTLES

CHELONIOIDEA

LOVE OUR OCEAN | 89 | YOUNG OCEAN EXPLORERS

TURTLE RESCUE

Five out of seven of the world's sea turtle species have been spotted in New Zealand waters, but turtles don't always like it this far south!

Turtles travel south to New Zealand on something called the East Auckland Current, which sweeps past the tropics before it hits New Zealand. It's all good when sea turtles arrive in our waters in the summer, when the ocean is at its warmest... but when winter arrives and the water cools... Brrrr!! No wonder turtles are sometimes washed up on our beaches during winter and spring storms – the cold weather's a bit of a shock to them!!

Turtles can also wash up on beaches when they're ill from all the plastic they eat – it's so sad! However they end up beached, sick turtles need help! I'm so glad there are people out there that can help my favourite animals!

Poor Stacey

Vet check at NZ Centre of Conservation and Medicine (Auckland Zoo)

Rehab at Kelly Tarlton's Sea Life Aquarium

Yahoo-back in the ocean

TURTLE HOTLINE 0800 DOC HOT

Learning about the problems in the ocean can be really sad. When you're young, it can feel like you can't change anything.

Actually, that's not true! Young people can change the world. Have you heard of the saying that goes 'think globally, act locally'? Once you know about global problems like plastic in the ocean, you can make sure there's less plastic in YOUR corner of the ocean.

Even picking up rubbish makes a real difference. Did you know that maybe 80% of the plastic in the ocean comes directly from the shore? This means it's come from drains and rivers, or just blown out to sea.

My baby brother Lucas made my family change what we do with rubbish! Once he saw my school project about turtles and plastic, he wouldn't let us go anywhere without picking up plastic! He also caused us to think about how much rubbish we create.

There's an amazing true story about a New Zealand high school student, Samara Nicholas, who with her class was inspired to make a difference, while working on a school project to establish a marine reserve in the Whangarei Harbour. Their dream became a reality and two marine reserves were set up. It was the first time in the world that a class of school kids had done this! Samara went on to set up a programme called EMR (Experiencing Marine Reserves) which takes school kids and community groups from all around New Zealand to experience marine reserves for themselves. It was through one of their programmes at Mahurangi College and a requirement to put experience into action that I got the idea for my school project that inspired Young Ocean Explorers!
Read more at: http://emr.org.nz

Dad reckons that kids like us can make a huge difference, first by being a great influence on our families and friends, like Lucas, and then by dreaming big about changing the world, like Samara!

MAKE A DIFFERENCE

Samara Nicholas

My baby bro Lucas

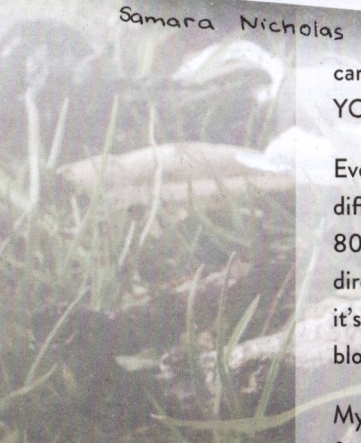

AOTEAROA - NEW ZEALAND
HAURAKI GULF
LITTLE BARRIER
AUCKLAND

MANGO
SHARKS
SELACHII

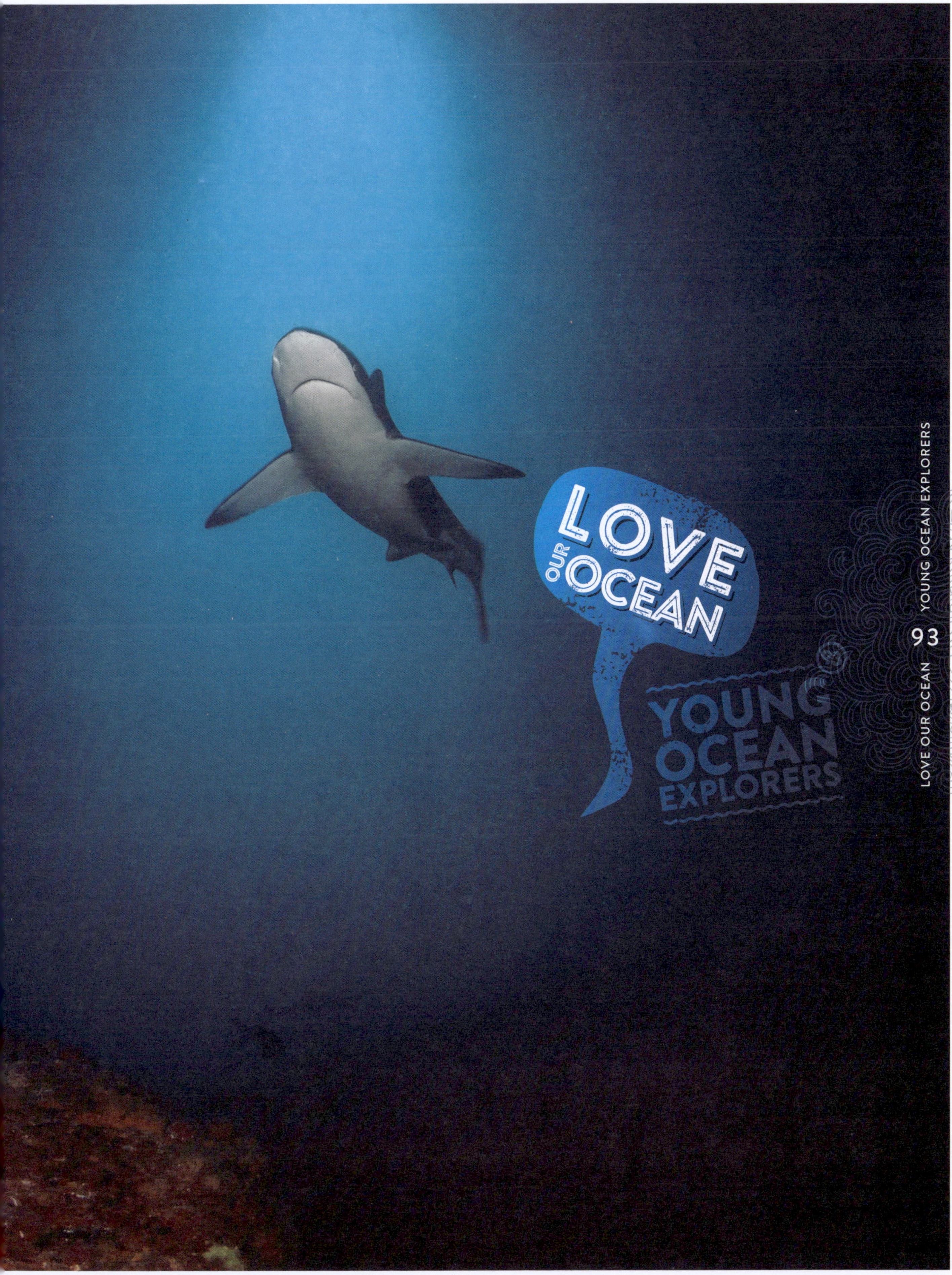
LOVE OUR OCEAN
YOUNG OCEAN EXPLORERS

MANGO SHARKS

SELACHII

"You're standing on a boat above a big underwater rock that is known to attract lots of sharks. Do you jump in?"

Haha - watch out for the sharks Dad!

a) Immediately
b) Yes (but only because your dad and his mate, who is a total shark expert, are already in the water grinning up at you.)
c) NO WAY!

Answer: B !!!

OK, so I might have swum with my first shark while we were out filming our 'stingrays' episode recently, but I'm still not completely comfy with them. Actually, my dad has told me that even he was scared of sharks when he was a kid: after seeing a movie called Jaws he was so freaked out by the idea of sharks that he would even get scared when he was swimming alone in his family's swimming pool. It's crazy how your brain can get stuck on unrealistic ideas when you don't know a lot about something! Now he knows heaps about sharks and swims with them all the time...

AND HE LOVES IT!

Dad had chosen this shark hotspot in the Hauraki Gulf so that we could check out some sharks doing their thing in the ocean ecosystem. His mate, Craig Thorburn, was with us which was so cool – Craig has swum with sharks hundreds of times and, like Dad, he really loves them. Craig even has a favourite shark species – the mako (one of the fastest fish in the ocean). Dad likes bronze whalers, although he says they can be a pain when you're spearfishing, especially if you're towing fish like kingfish or butterfish – bronze whalers will try to steal them! He reckons they must taste like shark candy.

Galapagos Shark

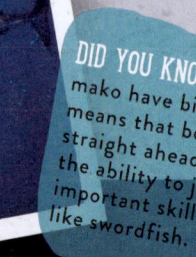

DID YOU KNOW?... Sharks like the mako have binocular vision; this means that both eyes can look straight ahead like ours, giving mako the ability to judge distances – an important skill for catching prey like swordfish.

Mako Shark

LOVE OUR OCEAN | YOUNG OCEAN EXPLORERS

94

Dad and Craig got in the water and once I'd sussed out that they weren't losing any body parts, I got in too. It was Fish City down there – there were trevally and kahawai everywhere! Bronze whalers love eating school fish like kahawai and trevally (as well as rays and other small sharks) so this was the perfect place to find one – or so we thought!

DID YOU KNOW?... Sharks can detect tiny electrical currents. If you had a wire running right around New Zealand and connected it to a 1.5 volt torch battery, the shark could detect the electrical current flowing through the wire.

HERE SHARKY SHARKY SHARKY!

Galapagos sharks look almost identical to bronze whalers.

After a few hours of looking for a Bronzy we got so desperate that we even tried banging two rocks together to bring one around. (Sharks have an incredible sense of hearing.) Believe me, it feels weeiiird to try to attract the most feared animal on the planet! But even trying every trick in the book, we were out of luck; our 'sharks' episode was going to be sharkless.

Although we hadn't seen any sharks on 'fish patrol' today, I asked Craig about something I'd heard – that by eating fish, sharks help to keep ecosystems healthy. I figured that this didn't make sense – wouldn't they eat up all the fish? Craig said that sharks tend to go for the old, slow and weak fish, which helps keep the remaining fish population healthy. Sharks also stop the numbers of some fish species from getting out of control. If there were too many fish grazing on seaweed, for example, those plants would get grazed down to nothing!

Teeth are really important for sharks and Craig showed me the jaw from a bronze whaler. It was soooo cool – I could fit my head in it! He explained how different sharks have different types of teeth that are really good at catching their favourite food. Great white sharks have particularly sharp 'knives' designed for cutting pieces of flesh from seals and larger animals. Tiger shark teeth can cut through turtle shells. Bronze whalers have teeth that are like 'knives and forks' – perfect for catching fish: the bottom teeth grip like forks while the top teeth chomp down like knives.

The sharks may have been playing hard to find, but as we headed back home we were in for an amazing surprise. All of a sudden, the glassy calm ocean erupted as a whale surfaced next to the boat! Dad jumped into the water to film as the Bryde's whale swam around a school of tiny fish. It was blowing bubbles to scare them into a tighter and tighter ball so it could swallow them up with one scoop of its huge mouth. Dad was so excited that he was squealing as the whale swam past him three times!

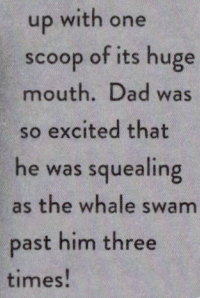

Blue shark – smile for the camera

DID YOU KNOW?... If you roll a shark on its back it goes to sleep?

MANGO
SHARKS
SELACHII

sand tiger sharks teeth look pretty impressive

DID YOU KNOW?... Sharks' skin is covered in really tiny teeth that you can only see with a microscope. Each of these teeth is unique to each species of shark. In the mako these tiny skin teeth (called denticles) actually help the shark swim faster.

It's so funny that people will spend all their time in the ocean freaking out about sharks, and here we were spending all day looking for them, but unable to find even one – instead we found one of the ocean's gentle giants!

With all those teeth, sharks may always seem a little bit scary. But they're beautiful, and as I learned, they have an important part to play in the ocean ecosystem. Although it might sound weird to you (actually, it still sounds a bit weird to me too) next time I'm hoping we actually find one!

Meet the Gurus

SHARK GURU

CRAIG THORBURN

Nationality? New Zealander.

Do you have any hobbies? Diving, snorkelling, fishing, sailing.

Why did you decide to be a scientist? I grew up fishing, sailing and snorkelling in New Zealand. The underwater world was just amazing. Guys like Wade Doak, Roger Grace and Jacques Cousteau made the underwater world seem like the best ever adventure!

How long have you been working in science? 25 years.

Did you enjoy school and did you find learning easy? I really enjoyed school, but found learning really hard. What I was good at was telling stories; I was never short of imagination.

Who do you work for? Merlin Entertainments Group who own Kelly Tarlton's SEA LIFE Aquarium as well as a number of aquariums in Australia and worldwide.

What do you do there? I am the senior curator for Asia, Australia and New Zealand. This means I am responsible for the happiness of all the animals in our care. We design new displays and environments, collect marine life to tell stories about, and research and figure out the best ways to take care of all of our animals. We also help with marine conservation and education. It is a really cool job.

What is your favourite animal? Without a doubt it's the mighty mako shark. To me they are the ultimate smart shark: fast, agile, not too dangerous and fun to be with (if you are careful and experienced).

What is the best part of your job? Marine life is so rewarding to work with, whether it is rescuing a turtle or even a stingray, or breeding penguins and endangered sharks!

Why do you like the ocean so much? I like swimming in it and seeing other animals the best; it is like flying but underwater, you feel weightless. It is also a challenging place where you can find time to think; and sometimes just open your eyes and gaze at another world.

Knowing what you know now, what's one piece of advice you would give kids about the ocean? Get into it! Less than one person in every 100 ever learns to dive, so do something special; be in the top one percent of adventurers and explore a unique world that is so easy to access.

DID YOU KNOW?... Around the world there are over 400 species of shark. Around 70 species are found in New Zealand waters, ranging from the tiny pygmy shark to the giant whale shark.

MANGO

SHARKS

SELACHII

LOVE OUR OCEAN · 99 · YOUNG OCEAN EXPLORERS

MARINE RESERVES

I love snorkeling in marine reserves – there is SOOOOO much more to see than in other places! This is because everything in a marine reserve is protected. That's right – no fishing! But that doesn't mean reserves are bad news if you love fishing.

CHECK OUT THESE COOL FACTS...

Marine reserves actually increase fish stocks in the rest of the ocean! The bigger a fish or crayfish gets – the more babies it has! Marine reserves are full of large fish that've been able to reach maturity. They make lots more babies than the average-sized snapper that are found elsewhere around the coast!

New Zealand is home to one of the world's first marine reserves! Cape Rodney-Okakari Point (Goat Island) Marine Reserve was opened in 1977. Hundreds of thousands of people visit Goat Island every year!

When Goat Island was started in 1977, it was just the same as every other bit of coastline nearby – there weren't many fish! Now, there are heaps!

When marine reserves are set up, humans don't really have to do anything (except stop fishing, of course!) Nature slowly builds up fish numbers as the ecosystem gets back into balance!

Marine guru, Mr Wade Doak, calls marine reserves 'wet libraries.' They're places kids can visit to see what a healthy bit of ocean looks like. It's such a cool idea to learn about fish by swimming with them, not just reading about them!

Blue maomao

That's a lot of fish!

In a recent study, Mr Adam Smith used footage from underwater cameras to count snapper inside and outside of marine reserves. "We found 20 times more large snapper in Leigh Marine Reserve than in nearby areas outside the reserve."

...DO YOU KNOW WHERE YOUR NEAREST MARINE RESERVE IS?

PHOTOGRAPHY
Meet the GURU

RICHARD "DIVERDICK" ROBINSON

Nationality? Kiwi.

Do you have any hobbies? Collecting old cameras and working on old cars.

Why did you decide to be an underwater photojournalist? Even though New Zealand is surrounded by the sea and everyone loves the beach and fishing, not many people know what's going on below the waves. Science can be confusing and complicated, so I like to take photographs in a way that helps explain things to kids like you.

How long have you been a photographer? My grandfather was a photographer like me and gave me a camera when I was very young, so I have been taking photographs as long as I can remember.

Where do you work? At www.depth.co.nz

What do you do? I like to tell people I'm an underwater photojournalist. A photojournalist takes pictures that tell stories about important things happening in the world. I take pictures that tell stories about important things happening in the sea.

What does a normal day at work look like to you? Most people think I spend all my time on boats, sailing around New Zealand, diving and taking pictures. I do get to do this some of the time, but most of the time is spent in front of a computer; researching stories, editing pictures and dreaming up the next adventure.

What is your favourite animal? Sharks. The bigger the shark the more I like them. I don't tell my mum when I'm off photographing sharks - she thinks I'm crazy.

What do you want to achieve through your work? I want to take pictures that are beautiful and powerful, but also educate people that our oceans are fragile and need to be looked after.

Best part of your job? Everything.

Worst part of your job? Washing wetsuits and cleaning camera gear.

When did you learn to swim/snorkel? About the same time I started taking photographs. I always wanted to be a diver and I loved everything about the sea. Because of this, my family gave me the nickname DiverDick.

102 YOUNG OCEAN EXPLORERS | LOVE OUR OCEAN

SNORKELLING'S FUN!

"HEY THERE! Are you new to snorkelling? That's so cool! Here are a few tips from what Dad taught me..."

GETTING READY!

Got a new mask? It's really important to give the glass on the inside a good clean with toothpaste. Rub it around with your finger then clean it off. This takes a film off the glass, making it easier to keep clean.

Eww yuck - I hate doing this

Here's the gross part – each time you use your mask, spit inside it and wipe it around with your finger! This stops it fogging up... there's no point in going snorkelling if you can't see anything!

When you put your mask on, make sure it fits tight against your face.

If you've got a wetsuit, they are good for buoyancy and also keeping you warm – but don't worry if you don't have one.

Put on your fins (aka flippers) while you're sitting a few metres away from the edge of the water – this makes sure that any waves don't sweep away any of your gear.

IN THE WATER!

Always snorkel in pairs and with an adult – it's safer and more fun!

If you're new to snorkelling, using a boogie board to rest on is a good idea. Try to relax and if you get tired – don't panic!

Let an adult know where you're going and how long you'll be.

Keep an eye on how far out you're heading... don't swim too far. The destination is only half of the journey. Leave plenty of energy to swim back!

103

LOVE OUR OCEAN | YOUNG OCEAN EXPLORERS

GLOSSARY

Fish anatomy diagram labels: DORSAL FIN, LATERAL LINE, CAUDAL FIN (TAIL), EYE, NOSTRIL, PECTORAL FIN, MOUTH, GILL COVER, PELVIC FIN, ANAL FIN

CARNIVOROUS – a plant or animal that only eats the meat of animals.

CETACEAN – any whale, dolphin or porpoise.

CRUSTACEAN – a group of animals that includes crabs, lobsters, crayfish, shrimp, krill and barnacles.

ECOSYSTEM – a group of plants, animals and other living things that live in the same place and help each other to survive.

ENDEMIC – found only in one particular country. Species that are endemic to New Zealand are only found in New Zealand.

EXCLUSIVE ECONOMIC ZONE/EEZ – an ocean area that is looked after by a particular country.

FILTER-FEEDERS – animals that feed by sucking in water and filtering it to take out anything that can be eaten.

FRONDS – leaves that are long and divided up into different shapes. The fronds of kelps are often ribbon shaped.

HARVESTING – taking food to be eaten. Usually harvesting takes place at a certain time of year, when that food is ripe or able to be taken without negative effects on an ecosystem.

KINA – sea urchins. Kina is the Maori name for sea urchins.

KIWIS – New Zealanders often talk about themselves as being kiwis.

PARASITES – animals or plants that survive by taking advantage of another animal or plant. Parasites may harm their victims, but they do not usually kill them.

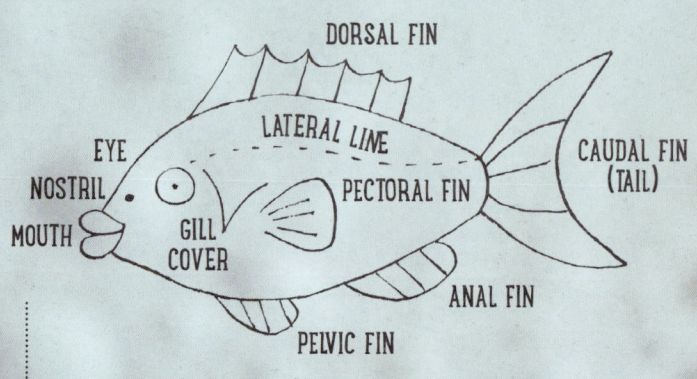

PHOTOSYNTHESIZE – to make energy from sunlight. Plants absorb the sun's rays and store that energy as sugar molecules, then use the energy to grow.

PHYTOPLANKTON – tiny creatures that live in the top layer of the oceans, making food out of the sun's rays. They are at the bottom of the food chain.

PIPI – a shellfish with a long white oval shell.

PREDATOR – an animal that eats another animal to survive.

SEDIMENTATION – a build-up of small particles that makes the water dirty.

SHELLFISH – animals that live in water and have a hard shell. Some shellfish, such as pipis and cockles, are molluscs (related to slugs and snails). Others, such as crabs and shrimp, are arthropods (related to insects).

STIPE – the stem that grows out of the base of a kelp plant. Fronds grow out of the stipe.

SUSTAINABLY – in a way that does not damage the health of a species or ecosystem.

TEMPERATE – moderately warm temperatures. The temperate parts of Earth are usually considered to be found between the tropics and the polar regions.

ZOOPLANKTON – a group of plankton that feed on phytoplankton. Most zooplankton are only visible through a microscope but some are larger, such as jellyfish.

105

LOVE OUR OCEAN · YOUNG OCEAN EXPLORERS

KICKSTARTER

While Young Ocean Explorers was screening on the kids TV show 'What Now,' we heard about teachers using our videos in their classes, saying it was brilliant for helping hook kids into learning about the ocean.

It got Dad thinking about how cool it would be if every school in New Zealand and the Cook Islands could get a copy of the Young Ocean Explorers book and DVD... that's nearly 2560 schools!

Thank you so much everybody without your incredible generosity this never would have happened! Thanks! Riley

About this time, Dad was the guest speaker at a meeting, telling them about Young Ocean Explorers. Somebody from the Bobby Stafford-Bush Foundation was there. He talked to Dad afterwards and said, what you're doing sounds incredible. We want to help you get this book and DVD into schools.

WOW, that was so amazing... they provided most of the money we needed to achieve this. All we needed to do was raise the last $20,000. (Eeek!!) Dad thought running a Kickstarter campaign would be a good way to do it – that's a really cool website where you can list your idea for a project and people can donate money to get it going.

Our Kickstarter campaign went really well and quickly raised $20,000... then people kept giving... until it reached $40,202!

LOVE OUR OCEAN

Unbelievable! People were incredibly generous and really wanted to see this happen!!!
We were so excited that people had been so supportive and really believed that Young Ocean Explorers could make a difference.

These are some of the amazing people and groups who have joined us in making this happen:

$100 OR MORE:
Andrew and Rachel McCulloch; Andy Gibson; Andy Brandy Casagrande IV; Angeleen Connolly; Beth Davidow; Billy Matheson; Brian Armstrong; Craig and Lauren Henderson and Family; Debs and Caleb; Deirdre Tollestrup; Denis Adams and Trish Mahon-Adams; Fisheye Films; Gary and Cheryl Mailand; Gary and Michelle Diprose and Family; Henderson Family; Jacinda Lilly; Jacqui Scott; Joyce Hawkesby; Julian Currin and Lief Pearson; Kenny Favel; Martin and Kim Axtens; Michael McCleary; Melika King; Neil Marsh; Noeleen Hathaway; NZ Dolphin Underwater and Adventure Club; Piet; Ray Bremer; Rich Borret; Robin McCullough; Roddy McKerchar; Rosina Lisker; Shaz Hathaway; Sue Cameron; The Pelan Family; Willy; Yukon Dive - Poor Knights

$500 OR MORE:
Angela and Jeremy Richardson; Axel; Dr Sheelagh James; Jeanette and Wally Martin; Len Ward; Snedden Family; Tony Forlong; Yuin Khai Foong

OTHERS:
Tony and Heather Gibson (Riley's grandparents); Hauraki Gulf forum; Environmental Initiative Fund (Auckland Council)

Thank you also to the businesses and organisations who have generously supported us in this journey.

This is my family (from left to right) – Dad, me, Alana, Dylan, Lucas and Mum

The Hathaway family would really like to thank everyone who has been part of this amazing journey so far and would especially like to thank the following:

Craig Henderson; Rees Morley; Stephanie Chamberlain; Carlene Managh; Richard Robinson; Grant Liebezeit; Jamie McDell and their families.

The Gurus – Wade Doak; Dan Godoy; Dr Roger Grace; Dr Tim Haggit; Dr Agnes LePort; Adam Smith; Dr Karen Stockin; Craig Thorburn; Dr Tom Trnski and Dr Ingrid Visser

Brian and Noeleen Hathaway; Tony and Heather Gibson; Brian and Paddy Stafford-Bush; John and Julie Dawson; Gary and Michelle Diprose; Jack Ralston; Matt Cowie; Phil Gaze; Margaret Kenning; Andy Kent; Dean Martin; Scott Unsworth; Angeleen Willocks; All the team at 'What Now'; Rebecca Fawcett; Gem Knight; Ronnie Taulafo; Adam Percival; Phil Guyan; Jomine Ayers; Julia Bloore; Erin Carpenter; Josh Couch; Thelma Wilson; Gary Winger; Simon O'Shaughnessy; Raewyn Pattemore; Craig Pritchard; Jonno Maskell; Greig and Sascha Brebner; Paul Carstensen; Simon Carter; Cam Hooper; Margaret and Peter Howard; Denis and Trish Adams; Samara Nicholas; Mark Mitchell MP; David Macleod; Tony Hafoka; Lily Kozmian-Ledward; Robert Marc Lehmann; Paul Caiger; Anna Berthelsan; Kate Malcolm; Jeroen Jonejan; the awesome team at Dive Tutukaka; Petra Bagust; Seaquel Wetsuits; Bill Ballantine; Darryl and Gillian Torckler; Brian and Julie George; Tony and Jenny Enderby; Jill Corkin; Andrew Cowie; Delwyn Dickie; Arthur Cozens; John Montgomery; Brady Doak; David and Jeanette Thomas; Ivan and Christina Blackwell; Krista Rankmore; Daniel DeJong;

Mels Barton; Mandy Kupenga; Pete Bethune; Shelley Campbell and the SPBT team; Josiah Diprose; Durham Pearce; Ariki Pearson; Sam Judd; Trevor and Jan Yaxley; Clinton Duffy; Andy Casagrande IV; Matt Ferraro; Carrie Vonderhaar; Stephanie Gibson; Tina Broadbent; Brijana Cato; Kate Elton; John Fellet; Dr Rochelle Constantine; Marcel Currin; Katrina Goddard; Kevin Denholm; Andrew Penny; Ulrick Petersen; Mark Kitteridge; Noelene Douglas; Matt Roser; Pat Swanson; Murray Thom; Kate Port; Tim Richie; Cath Dunsford; Sarah Dwyer; Jochen Zaeschmar; Kate Madsen; Ben Dugdale; Tracey Martin MP; Phil Warbrick; Rhys Sutton; Allen Entwisle; Bronwen Golder; David Garrett; Karen Gibson; Michael Walker; Lyndsay Simpkin; Tiff Stewart; Joel Harper; Eli Martinez; James McGinlay; Dave Moran; Tarx Morrison; Gordon McKerchar; Malachi Tomey; Richard Nauck; James Heyward; Tim Higham; Sharlene Merton; Roddy McKerchar; Jessica Ngatai; Rachel O'Malley; Helen Pearson; Natalie Usmar; Phil McGowan; Amanda Robinson; Scott Tindale; Adam and Lexi Waterhouse; Phil Hathaway; Chris Mace; Mark and Katie Gatt; Snells Beach Spearfishing Club; Snedden family; Julie Green; Len Ward; Sheelagh James; Terry Axford

To those who believed in our vision 4 years ago – this would never have happened without your belief:

Geoff and Mandy Burne; Warwick and Katie Rhodes; Tony Forlong; David Knight; Hamish Alexander; Bill and Laurel Collins; Shaz Hathaway; Linda Brereton; Steve Hudson; Scottie McKinnon; Gabriel Mueller; William Row; Matt Wilmot; Sigman Spath; Gordon and Nola Maskell; Matt and Jacinda Lily; Daniel Chapman; Paul and Liz Blackwell; Paul Bull; Julie Green; Leigh Hopper; Stuart and Ginny Henderson; Bruce Smith; Robin Brooke; Darryl and Bridget Soljan; Greg Fleming; Robin Shingleton

Young Ocean Explorers TV Series:
Producer/Director: Craig Henderson (Symphony)
Producer/Writer: Steve Hathaway
Camera Operators: Matt Gerrand and Catriona Goodey
Camera Assistant: Frederick Muller
Editors: Julian Currin and Alex Mitchell
Sound mixes: Native Audio
Color Grading: Dave Gibson (Toybox)
Show Pilot Camera: Jared Brandon
Show Pilot Editing: Steven Baker

All photos by Richard Robinson unless stated otherwise. All credited photos below are snapshots unless stated as a main photo. None of the Gurus photos are credited.
M (Main photo) - T (Top) - R (Right)
C (Centre) - L (Left) - B (Bottom)
Pg 6 M Brijana Cato; Pg 13 R Craig Henderson; Pg 19 T Paul Caiger; R Paul Caiger; Pg 20 Paul Caiger; Pg 22 T Richard Robinson; C Richard Robinson; Pg 34-41 All photos © Orca Research Trust, Dr Ingrid Visser; Pg 36 B Robert Marc Lehmann; Pg 38 M Eli Martinez; B Steve Hathaway; Pg 39 T Eli Martinez; B Mazdak Radjainia; Pg 51 T Brijana Cato; R Jane Healy; Pg 61 T Dr Ingrid Visser; Pg 84 M Chris Fallows/Apexpredators.com; Brijana Cato; Pg 87 Gary Diprose; Pg 90 T Department of Conservation, Te Tai Kauri / Kauri Coast Office; C Jane Healy; BR Craig Pritchard; Pg 99 L Jane Healy; R Dan Godoy; Pg 100 T Jane Healy; B Craig Pritchard; Pg 102 C Quentin Bennett

YOUNG OCEAN EXPLORERS: LOVE OUR OCEAN

Written by Steve and Riley Hathaway in collaboration with Stephanie Chamberlain

www.youngoceanexplorers.co.nz

Hang out with us on...

Published by Underwater Promotions Ltd
PO Box 61 Snells Beach, New Zealand 0942
First published February 2015

ISBN 978-0-473-30922-0

Design and production by Rees Morley – Morley Design Group

Photography by Richard Robinson

Illustrations by Jamie McDell

Printed in China

Copyright © Underwater Promotions Ltd
All rights reserved. No part of this publication may be reproduced, stored in a retrieval system, or transmitted in any form or by any means without the prior written permission of the publisher.